Gender and Social Movements

THE GENDER LENS SERIES

Series Editors

Judith A. Howard
University of Washington

Barbara Risman
North Carolina State University

Joey Sprague
University of Kansas

The Gender Lens Series has been conceptualized as a way of encouraging the development of a sociological understanding of gender. A "gender lens" means working to make gender visible in social phenomena; asking if, how, and why social processes, standards, and opportunities differ systematically for women and men. It also means recognizing that gender inequality is inextricably braided with other systems of inequality. The Gender Lens series is committed to social change directed toward eradicating these inequalities. Originally published by Sage Publications and Pine Forge Press, all Gender Lens books are now available from AltaMira Press.

BOOKS IN THE SERIES

Yen Le Espiritu, *Asian American Women and Men: Labor, Laws, and Love*

Judith A. Howard and Jocelyn A. Hollander, *Gendered Situations, Gendered Selves: A Gender Lens on Social Psychology*

Michael A. Messner, *Politics of Masculinities: Men in Movements*

Judith Lorber, *Gender and the Social Construction of Illness*

Scott Coltrane, *Gender and Families*

Myra Marx Ferree, Judith Lorber, and Beth B. Hess, editors, *Revisioning Gender*

Pepper Schwartz and Virginia Rutter, *The Gender of Sexuality: Exploring Sexual Possibilities*

Francesca M. Cancian and Stacey J. Oliker, *Caring and Gender*

M. Bahati Kuumba, *Gender and Social Movements*

Toni M. Calasanti and Kathleen F. Slevin, *Gender, Social Inequalities, and Aging*

Gender and Social Movements

M. Bahati Kuumba

ALTAMIRA
PRESS

A Division of Rowman and Littlefield Publishers, Inc.
Walnut Creek • Lanham • New York • Oxford

ALTAMIRA PRESS
A Division of Rowman & Littlefield Publishers, Inc.
1630 North Main Street, #367
Walnut Creek, CA 94596
www.altamirapress.com

Rowman & Littlefield Publishers, Inc.
A wholly owned subsidiary of The Rowman & Littlefield Publishing Group, Inc.
4501 Forbes Boulevard, Suite 200
Lanham, MD 20706

PO Box 317
Oxford
OX2 9RU, UK

British Library Cataloguing in Publication Information Available

Library of Congress Cataloging-in-Publication Data

Kuumba, M. Bahati.
   Gender and social movements / M. Bahati Kuumba.
      p. cm.—(Gender lens)
   Includes bibliographical references and index.
   ISBN 0-7591-0187-6 (alk. paper)—ISBN 0-7591-0188-4 (pbk. : alk. paper)
   1. Sex role. 2. Social movements. 3. Social change. I. Title. II. Series.

HQ1075 .K88 2001
303.48′4—dc21

2001022781

Printed in the United States of America

♾™ The paper used in this publication meets the minimum requirements of American National Standard for Information Sciences—Permanence of Paper for Printed Library Materials, ANSI/NISO Z39.48–1992.

CONTENTS

ACKNOWLEDGMENTS

I am indebted to countless individuals, on multiple levels, for support and assistance during the life of this project. Although I am unable to list the names of every individual, my appreciation extends to all who contributed to this collective effort.

Let me begin by acknowledging the loving womb of my family and friends who kept me whole and grounded throughout this endeavor. I continue to be guided by the living spirits of Arthalia and Manny Jackson, Virginia Jackson, and Essie Edwards. Thanks also to my daughter, Tendayi Nia Evalia Kuumba, for having such patience with her workaholic mom, and to my blood sister, Talibah (Adrienne) Nyaako, for her wit and wisdom. I received unflinching assistance from Shirley and Roy Logan, Jacqueline Edwards, Eva Brown, and Dwayne Edwards. Not at all least, I extend "much love" to my partner and rock, Sobukwe Shukura.

The list of the many other friends who supported me throughout this endeavor would be longer than the book itself. I would be remiss, however, if I did not give mention to my sisters in struggle: Femi Ajanaku, Sonda Tamarr Allen, Ann Bennett Crossley, Tumika Daima, Ona Alston-Dosunmu, Claudia and Joy Moguel, Paulette Murphy, Janet Reed, Regine Zekora Romain, and Bonnie Stewart. I can't forget the brothers in struggle (and I *do* mean struggle): Gerry Eastman, Curtis Haynes Jr., Doug Koritz, Rickie Smith, Ron Stewart, and Fanon Wilkins.

I am grateful to AltaMira Press, Mitch Allen, and the Gender Lens Editorial Collective—Judith Howard, Barbara Risman, Mary Romero, and Judy Sprague—for believing in the possibilities of this project. In particular, Judy Howard's encouragement, as well as her thoughtful and prompt response to every draft, was a motivating force in this book coming to fruition. Additionally, I appreciate Peter Labella for support in the early stages of the manuscript. I thank my *dream team*, particularly Rose Brewer (for including me on hers) and other colleagues who read and insightfully commented on the manuscript at different stages of its life. These scholars include (but are certainly not limited to): Dionne Jones, Walda Katz Fishman, Sara Slavin, and Assata Zerai. The research assistance that I received from Amber Faulkner, Uchenna Smith, and Nava Yeshoalul was invaluable and evident in every one of the pages that follows.

This project was also aided by the generous support that I received from the State University of New York United University Professions (UUP), Buffalo State College's Academic Affairs and Division of Natural and Social Sciences, and the African American Research Foundation.

I am eternally grateful to my old academic home, Buffalo State College, for providing such a nurturing environment. In particular, I thank members of the Sociology Department, Resurgent City Research Group (RESURGE), the Office of Equity and Campus Diversity, and the African and African American Studies Interdisciplinary Unit. Equal gratitude is extended toward my new academic home, Spelman College, into which I have been welcomed with open arms.

(Selected events and dates)

Civil Rights/Black Power Movements

Gender Parallelism, 1955–1965

1955   Montgomery Bus Boycott begins, initiated by the Women's Political Council (WPC), Montgomery, Alabama, December 5

1957   Southern Christian Leadership Council (SCLC) founded

1958   Ella Baker becomes Executive Secretary of SCLC

1960   Student Nonviolent Coordinating Committee (SNCC) founded, April 16
Sit-ins initiated in Greensboro, North Carolina, February 1

1961   Freedom Rides organized by the Congress on Racial Equality (CORE)
SNCC Voter Registration Project, McComb, Mississippi

1962   Formation of Cambridge Nonviolent Action Committee (CNAC), Cambridge, Maryland

1963   March on Washington

1964   Freedom Summer, Mississippi
Mississippi Freedom Democratic Party (MFDP) founded, April 26
Civil Rights Act passed
SNCC Women's Office Strike
SNCC's Waveland Meeting—"Women in the Movement" Position Paper disseminated, Waveland, Mississippi

Gender Polarization, 1966–1997

1966   Black Panther Party Formed, Oakland, California
Ruby Doris Smith Robinson elected as SNCC Executive Secretary

1967   National Welfare Rights Organization formed

1968   Third World Women's Alliance founded
All African People's Revolutionary Part formed

1973   The National Black Feminist Organization founded, New York

1974   Elaine Brown becomes Chairperson of the Black Panther Party (highest office held by a woman)
The Combahee River Collective formed, Boston, Massachusetts
African Women's Conference (sponsored by the Congress of Afrikan People), Rutgers University

1975   Black Women's United Front formed

1979   Black Women and Liberation Movements Conference, Howard University, Washington, D.C.

1980   National Black United Front (NBUF) founded
        National Black Independent Political Party (NBIPP) founded
        All African Women's Revolutionary Union (AAWRU) formed, women's wing
        of the All African People's Revolutionary Party
1995   Million Man March
1997   Million Women's March

Gender Transition, 1998–present
1998   – Black Radical and Black Radical Feminist Congress, June, Chicago, Illinois

Anti-Apartheid Movement

Gender Parallelism, 1950–1959
1952   The Defiance Campaign
1953   Pre-Federation of South African Women meeting of approximately fifty women,
        Port Elizabeth
1954   First Conference of Women held in Johannesburg, April
        FSAW founded
        ANC boycott of Bantu education and formation of "culture clubs"
1955   Women's Anti–Pass March on Pretoria, October 27
        Adoption of the Freedom Charter
        The Congress of Mothers Meeting
        South African Congress of Trade Unions (SACTU) formed
1956   FSAW-led anti-pass mobilization, August 9
        Second National Conference of the Federation of South African Women (FSAW),
        Johannesburg, August 11–12
1958   The Potato Boycott
1959   Cato Manor protests, Cato Manor, Durban, June
        Pan-Africanist Congress (PAC) founded

Gender Polarization/Asymmetry, 1960–1975
1960   The Sharpeville Massacre
        State of Emergency declared and banning of major liberation organizations
1961   *Umkhonto we Sizwe* ("Spear of the Nation") founded, armed wing of the ANC
1969   South African Students Organization (SASO) founded
1972   The Black People's Convention (BPC) founded, coalition of "Black Conscious-
        ness" organizations

1973   The Black Trade Union strikes in Durban
1975   Black Women's Federation founded

Gender Transition, 1975–1989
1976   Soweto Student Revolt, June 16
1977   The Inkatha Women's Brigade founded, May
       Black Women's Federation Banned
1978   Crossroads Resistance
       Azania People's Organization (AZAPO) founded
1981   United Women's Organization (UWO) founded
1983   The United Democratic Front (UDF) formed (unified over 700 community, trade
       union, cultural, women's and other organs)
1984   ANC's Year of Women
1986   Repeal of pass laws
1987   Revival of the Federation of South African Women (FEDSAW)

Gender Inclusion, 1990–Present
1990   Malibongwe Conference, Amsterdam, Netherlands
       Unbanning of the national liberation organizations
       ANC Women's League relaunched
       Mandela's release from prison
       Repeal of the Group Areas Act
1992   National Women's Coalition (WNC) formed, April
1994   National Election, ANC-led Government of National Unity
       Inaugurated, May 10
       Adoption of the Women's Charter for Effective Equity
       Commission on Gender Equality founded

The Social Movement as Gendered Terrain

I also knew from the beginning that having a woman be an executive of SCLC [Southern Christian Leadership Council] was not something that would go over with the male-dominated leadership. And then, of course, my personality wasn't right, in the sense I was not afraid to disagree with the higher authorities.

— Ella Baker
Civil rights activist

For a long time the women were not proper members of the ANC [African National Congress]. They only changed that in 1943 when the women were allowed to join properly. That was when the Women's League started.

— Frances Baard
South African anti-apartheid activist

Introduction

Ella Baker and Frances Baard, the women quoted above, are not generally familiar names despite the fact that they played significant roles in changing the world. Baker and Baard were leaders in the United States civil rights and South African anti-apartheid movements, respectively. They were both active in these movements for social change for more than fifty years and, together, participated in more than forty-five movement organizations. How is it possible for us to not be familiar with two individuals who provided leadership in very well known social movements over such a long period of time? It is possible because, as their quotes illustrate, their expe-

1

riences in these movements, both of which were primarily concerned with achieving racial equality and liberation, were affected by the fact that they were women.

From the 1940s through the 1980s, Frances Baard lent her energies to the struggle against the system of apartheid in South Africa that maintained racial segregation and inequality in all areas of life. She was a member of the most influential movement organizations of the day including the African National Congress (ANC), the Federation of South African Women (FSAW), and the South African Congress of Trade Unions (SACTU). During roughly that same period, Ella Baker served as a master strategist and participant in the civil rights movement to eliminate racial segregation and discrimination in the United States. She played a significant role in, and in some cases founded, some of its main organizations such as the National Association for the Advancement of Colored People (NAACP), the Southern Christian Leadership Council (SCLC), and the Student Nonviolent Coordinating Committee (SNCC). Both Baard and Baker were responsible for recruiting and coordinating thousands of people in these movements, organizing major programs, and directing overall strategy.

Along with millions of other individuals throughout history and in societies worldwide, Baard and Baker devoted great energies to changing their social conditions. The fact that their names are much less familiar than social movement leaders like Nelson Mandela and Martin Luther King Jr. does not reflect any lesser contribution to the movements on their part. Their relative invisibility is not coincidence, but is an illustration of one of many ways in which social movements can be gender biased. Not only do women and men experience the social realities that lead to the emergence of social movements differently, they often have differential experiences and play distinctive roles within social movements. Unearthing submerged stories of those like Baard and Baker, as a step toward understanding the broader gendered processes that impact movement processes, is a major objective of focusing a gender lens on social movements.

Social movements have the potential to reproduce as well as transform gender inequalities, structures, and belief systems. As such, they are dynamic processes to view through a "gender lens." In this book, I utilize a gendered mode of analysis through which to explore social movements which rests on the assumption that gender is a basic organizing principle in human society and that gender roles, relations, and inequalities impact social processes in complex ways. This lens makes gender visible and explores social processes and structures through assessing the impact of the socially constructed social categories, female and male (Howard and Hollander 1997). It involves taking the power, resource, and status differentials between women and men into account at each stage of the analysis. A gendered analysis places emphasis on gender differentiation in the broader social structures like economies and political systems, as well as on the impact of these forces on individual lives. It compels us to look beyond the surface of social realities and rethink basic assumptions by identifying and confronting inherent gender biases. The gender lens perspective also recognizes that gender systems, which generally disprivilege women relative to men in society, interact with other systems of inequality (Howard and Hollander 1997; Peterson and Runyan 1999).

This gendered analysis of the sociology of social movements uses as case studies the two twentieth-century social movements with which Ella Baker and Frances Baard are associated: the racial equality and national liberation movements in the United States and South Africa. While these two cases differ in many significant ways, they also have important parallels and commonalities. Using these cases offers an opportunity to illustrate the manner in which gender impacts both the study of and actual workings within social movements. I draw from these cases on multiple levels: macro, meso, and micro. On the macrolevel, I attempt to place these movements in their larger sociohistorical and structural contexts. I pay particular attention to the shifts in the gender, race, and class systems from which the movements arose and against which they struggled. On the mesolevel, I draw examples from the organizations, collectivities, and campaigns that served as the cornerstones of the movements. Lastly, on the microlevel, I rely on the biographies, life stories, and standpoint of women like Frances Baard and Ella Baker through which to tell the story.

Gender consciousness is currently transforming the way scholars study and theorize about social movements. In this book, I draw from and incorporate concepts and observations from contemporary gender-conscious social movement research that has emerged in the last three decades. In a reciprocal fashion, an additional objective of this study is to contribute to this body of scholarly work by furthering the development and application of a culturally contextualized, class-conscious, and gendered sociology of social movements.

What Are Social Movements and Why Study Them?

Ella Baker and Frances Baard contributed to changing the world through their active participation in social movements. Formally, social movements have been defined as conscious, organized, and collective actions to bring about or resist social change (Piven and Cloward 1979; West and Blumberg 1990). The twentieth century can boast of a wide range of social movements. The workers' rights and trade union movement was strong in the United States during the 1930s. Movements for national liberation and independence from foreign colonizing powers swept through Africa, Latin America, and Asia during the 1950s and 1960s. Socialist movements and struggles for economic justice were prevalent in Latin and Central America in the 1970s and 1980s. At the very least, most of us are generally familiar with the contemporary social movements in the United States that have sought rights for groups subjugated on the basis of race and/or ethnicity, gender, and sexuality such as the civil rights/Black Power, women's liberation, and gay and lesbian movements.

Despite the differences between them, social movements share some common characteristics that set them apart from other forms of collective behavior (Marx and McAdam 1994; Wood and Jackson 1982). Their definitive features include organization, consciousness, noninstitutionalized strategies, and prolonged duration. In contrast to riots, fads, and crowd behavior, social movements commonly exhibit some degree of structure and organization; a consciousness that links social discontent and grievances with a rationale or logic; noninstitutionalized action strategies; and a relatively long duration.

Scholars and activists have categorized social movements on the basis of various criteria and characteristics. One mode of classification rests on the political orientations of the movement. Those considered to the "left" end of the political spectrum are usually associated with progressive social change that will expand rights or equalize the distribution of social resources. Right-wing movements or countermovements seek to maintain or reestablish some threatened or past way of life like racial segregation or restricted access to abortion for women. Of the "leftist" movements, there are those that seek limited or reformist changes which leave the overall social system intact. These include the struggles to enact antidiscriminatory or equal opportunity legislation in the United States sought by the civil rights, pro-choice, and lesbian/gay rights movement organizations. Other movements and organizations are considered revolutionary or transformative because they desire sweeping and fundamental structural changes in the socioeconomic or political system of a society. Formations like the South African Communist Party or the Black Panther Party that sought to replace the system of capitalism with socialist relations fit into this category. Social movements for progressive change, both reformist and revolutionary, are important vehicles for social change that might not otherwise be achieved by a constituency that is restricted from participation in the established decision-making process.

While earlier scholars attributed the rise of social movements to the irrational reactions of alienated individuals to social changes or disruptions, contemporary approaches appreciate social movements as conscious and rational activities. Movement organizations and participants have belief systems and/or ideologies that explain the nature of the social condition they seek to change, justify particular strategies of action, and outline the anticipated outcomes or objectives. Movements often frame their grievances and claims of legitimacy within a language or system of thought that already has support and with which potential participants can relate. The civil rights movement utilized the language of human rights and individual freedoms, for example, ideals that already garnered great support in U.S. society.

People join and participate in movement efforts through the process of social movement mobilization (Klandermans 1984, 1986). Mobilization is dependent on a delicate balance between the existence of objective conditions that stimulate the emergence of protest movements and, on a more individual level, the subjective awareness and interpretation of these conditions. Periods of mass mobilization and heightened contention like the U.S. civil rights and anti-apartheid eras, when these objective and subjective aspects are in sync, have been termed "cycles of protest" according to Sidney Tarrow (1995). Theorists and activists often disagree among themselves about whether the objective conditions or subjective perception of those conditions are most important in fueling social resistance.

On a midrange level, organizational recruitment strategies can impact the probability and character of movement involvement. To different degrees, activists funnel their energies through formal and informal organizational networks, such as social movement organizations (SMOs) or communities of resistance. These entities can range from being highly structured and formal such as a political party to being a loosely connected group of individuals such as a community group or social network. Typically, social movement activities are coordinated simultaneously through a wide range of social movement types. For instance, the U.S. civil rights movement was reliant on the activities of the officially recognized social movement organizations like the Southern Christian Leadership Council (SCLC), a voter's rights organization with which Ella Baker was associated from 1957 to 1960. The movement was just as dependent, though, on the informal groupings and communication networks of individuals in local churches and neighborhoods with whom Baker communicated and strategized regularly.

The methods employed by social movement organizations and activists to raise awareness about an issue and impact some social condition are not adopted randomly. The conditions that surround the movement, the consciousness of the participants, and the ultimate objectives combine to determine the range of strategies and tactics that are available and appropriate. Since movements are, by definition, outside of the legitimate power structure, they usually rely on noninstutionalized or unconventional strategies to confront the power structure. Very often these tactics are defined as "illegal" from the power structure's point of view. In the early 1950s, Frances Baard participated in the Defiance Campaign in which people of African descent consciously disobeyed apartheid laws which required them to carry passes and not go into "Whites Only" areas.* While these actions were illegal from the South African government's point of view, they were effective methods of resistance open to movement participants. Social movement strategies can range from those that are nonviolent and peaceful, like the civil disobedience employed in the Defiance Campaign and early civil rights movement, to those that employ varying degrees of violence such as armed resistance and sabotage. The range of methods available in its "action repertoire" is constantly being expanded through the process of "tactical innovation" (Tarrow 1995).

Unlike many other types of collective actions, social movements are partially defined by their tendency toward prolonged duration and reverberating effects. The emergence, growth, and decline of social movements can span many decades. It often takes a long period of time for movements to achieve desired changes in the usually very stubborn established social order. In 1986, even after having been in the anti-apartheid movement for over forty years, Frances Baard is quoted as saying, "It takes a long time, this struggle, but it is coming, we just have to wait hopefully, and keep on fighting" (Baard 1986). The extended life of a movement is also evident in the duration of its structures. Social movement organizations can also be-

---

*Throughout the text, "African American" and "Black" will be used interchangeably to refer to people of African descent in the United States. In a similar fashion, "African" and "Black" will be used to refer to people of indigenous African descent in South Africa. The terms "European American" and "White" will be used to refer to people of European descent in the United States, while the only "Whites" will be used to refer to South Africans of European ancestry.

come institutionalized and live beyond the height of the movement. Although the National Association for the Advancement of Colored People (NAACP) was viewed as a radical organization in the movement during the 1940s, when Ella Baker served as field secretary, it is currently viewed as a legitimate and mainstream U.S. institution. Likewise, while the African National Congress (ANC) was a banned organization in 1960 by the Nationalist Government in South Africa, today it is the ruling political party. The aftershocks of movement efforts can also spill over into other collective struggles that adopt similar strategies and tactics.

Despite the fact that the effects of social movements surround us daily, we often take the impact they have had on our lives for granted. Many of the rights, freedoms, and protections that we enjoy daily are the direct result of collective movements for social change. The elimination of inhumane systems like slavery, the right for women and people of color to vote, workplace safety and labor standards, the passage of racial and gender equal opportunity legislation, and the independence from direct colonial control enjoyed by many of the world's nations can all be attributed to the success of social movements. Though social movements differ with respect to their specific objectives, the scope of social transformation that they seek, and their level of success, each has left its own indelible mark on the wider society as well as on the social movements to come.

The Sociological Study of Social Movements

Both scholars and activists have vested, but often different, interests in understanding and transmitting the lessons learned from the social movements of the past. From a scholarly perspective, the patterns and relationships observable from the legacy of social struggle offer insights that are used to understand contemporary movements and social insurgencies which are passed on in scholarly and popular publications, in presentations, and in the classroom. Activists, on the other hand, are often more interested in lessons from past movements that can be directly applied to movement building such as the ways in which past movements have mobilized participants, impacted the sentiment of the wider public, and successfully forged social change.

The study and investigation of social movements is a vibrant subfield in the discipline of sociology. This area of research and theorizing attempts to describe, explain, evaluate, and sometimes predict the various aspects of social resistance struggles. Wilson (1973) identified four major objectives of the sociological analysis of social movements:

1) the construction of a meaningful definition of social movements that distinguishes them from other forms of collective actions;
2) to understand the social conditions that give rise to movements and stimulate individual participation;
3) analysis of social movement structures and strategies of action; and
4) measurement of movement outcomes and consequences.

Many frameworks and models have been developed to better understand social movement emergence, organization, ideology, strategies, and outcomes. There are distinct theoretical approaches to social movements that each has its own set of assumptions, area(s) of emphasis, and level of analysis. They include paradigms that have been coined the collective behavior approach, resource mobilization model, political process model, and new social movement theory.

The *collective behavior approach*, a relatively early theoretical tradition, viewed social movements as the collective response to the individual alienation caused by the social strain and disruption of rapid social changes such as urbanization and industrialization (McAdam 1992; Smelser 1962). The *resource mobilization (RM) model* contrasts with this psychological orientation by stressing the importance of financial, organizational, and human resources available to a movement (McCarthy and Zald 1977; McAdam 1992). This model emphasizes the rationality and political nature of social movements. The *political process model* incorporates an appreciation for organizational resources, but it places more emphasis on the larger political context and structural configuration of the environment from which social resistance struggles emerge (Costain 1992; McAdam 1982). Shifts in the structure of political opportunities and constraints work with organizational resources and subjective perceptions to fuel social insurgency.

The most current theoretical trend, *new social movement theory*, steers away from the materialist approaches of the resource mobilization and political process models. This group of theories links a diverse range of concerns for symbolic, cultural, and ideational factors as crucibles for building sustained social protest movements (Buechler 1993; Melucci 1985). New social movement theorists emphasize subjective and symbolic aspects of social movements such as collective action frames and collective identities. Collective action frames, the ideas and interpretive analyses that link individuals to the movement, place movement objectives in a context with which potential participants are familiar and can agree. These frames often draw on existing belief or meaning systems in the society. Some of these models place emphasis on the salience of the collective sense that movement participants have of themselves, their collective identities (Snow and Benford 1988, 1992). Collective identities are constructions of a group "self" that are often forged in opposition to some external or "other" social group or category. These theoretical models and frameworks will be discussed in more detail in chapter 3.

The sociology of social movements has itself been influenced by social movements. Among other movement effects, the sociology of social movements is currently being transformed by the unfinished "feminist revolution" in the social sciences. As an outgrowth of the women's liberation movement of the late 1960s and 1970s, academic disciplines and theoretical paradigms have been revisited and transformed in ways that have filled in gaps and corrected sexist biases (Stacey and Thorne 1985). The heightened gender consciousness in the discipline has broadened and deepened the study of social movements. Before the gendered analysis of social movements, I discuss a social construct we usually take for granted—gender.

Gender: Contested Social Terrain

Gender is not as straightforward a concept as many believe. First, it is distinct from sex, the physical and physiological features that differentiate females and males. As opposed to being a biological designation, gender is a social construction—the differentiation and institutionalization of the expected characteristics, norms, and behaviors associated with being female or male in any specific social context. Gender also refers to the rank ordering of this social division, and subsequent statuses, on interlocking societal levels. The distinction between female and male spheres operates in the family, the economy, religion, political systems, educational institutions, and culture. It also interacts with other systems of social differentiation such as race, ethnicity, class, and sexuality. Defining and understanding the complex nature of gender as a social category has been contested terrain which, on one level, has been characterized by ideological struggles between essentialist and social constructionist conceptions of gender.

Essentialist Notions of Gender

Essentialist notions of gender argue that the distinctions and separate spheres assigned to women and men are inevitable and natural. The assumption of essential and innate differences between the sexes follows from the idea that females and males are biologically determined "natural" opposites (Hess and Ferree 1987). It portrays femininity and masculinity as dichotomized, mutually exclusive sets of behavioral or personality traits. Examples of gender polarization include the assumptions that men are automatically strong while women are weak or that women are overly emotional and intuitive versus the rationality and reason displayed by men. We could easily generate a list of contrasting characteristics and images associated with being female or male that would vary from society to society. Dichotomizing gendered natures justifies differential social roles and legitimates a division of labor and social spheres designated for women and men. Within sociology, the structural functionalist theoretical approach is most compatible with this normative division of labor by gender. In this scheme, "complimentarity" is viewed as necessary for the maintenance of social stability and equilibrium.

The essentialist understanding of gender difference has been criticized and hotly contested in recent decades (Gerson and Peiss 1985; Hess and Ferree 1987; Lopata and Thorne 1978; Stacey and Thorne 1985). For many scholars, this approach to gender is problematic because of its tendency to accept gender categories as inevitable and unchanging. Viewing gender characteristics and traits as biologically determined fails to explain or account for cross-cultural variation and changes over time in a society's gender system. This perspective also ignores the impact of structures and institutions in fashioning gender relations and the historical and political context within which gendered processes operate (Stacey and Thorne 1985). Finally, and most detrimental, this system of thought invariably privileges masculine traits and activities over feminine ones and upholds power and resource differences between women and men (Peterson and Runyan 1999). The essentialist notion of gender leaves gaps and unanswered questions. What about gender ambiguities or situations that do not fit squarely within the "boxes" of normative sex and gender role behavior? How do gender systems relate to other institutional arrangements in the society? What or whose interests are served by the established gender roles and patterns?

Constructionist Understandings of Gender

The development of frameworks and models that better capture the dynamism and multiple levels of gender has been an unfolding process. According to Hess and Ferree (1987) in *Analyzing Gender: A Handbook for Social Science Research*, "the study of men and women as such has moved through three distinct stages in just the past twenty years, from an emphasis on sex differences through preoccupation with sex roles to the centrality of gender" (Hess and Ferree 1987, 14). This latter emphasis goes beyond a simple identification of differences between women and men to an analysis of gender as a historically developed social system that operates interactively on social, political, economic, and cultural levels. Hess and Ferree explain further that

> gender is not a trait but a system for dividing people into distinct, nonoverlapping categories despite their natural variability on any particular characteristic and regardless of the inconsistency between features that we are all supposed to be definitive. (1987, 16)

Judith Lorber (1997[1993]) conceptualizes gender as an institution that acts as a key organizing principle in human social life. It not only defines a structured set of relations, statuses, and norms of behavior, this scheme incorporates (1) process, (2) stratification, and (3) structure.

Understanding gender as process focuses attention on the dynamic way that gendered patterns and relationships are continually constructed and reconstructed through human interaction. According to Lorber and other scholars who appreciate the dynamism of gender, we are constantly "doing gender," that is, creating, recreating, and reinforcing norms and behaviors associated with gender. We consistently use these gendered categories as basic assumptions in our analyses of the social world, other people, our relationships, and ourselves. Gerson and Piess (1985) refer to this as a process of negotiation in which the boundaries that demarcate the separate "genders" are contested and reinforced. Thinking of gender as process is helpful in that it stresses the fluid nature of gender, both transformed and transformative.

As a system of social stratification, gender involves the expressions of social inequality and hierarchy associated with women and men in societies. Differences in the allocation of resources, distribution of power, and opportunity structures are associated with the construction of gender categories. While the extent of inequality and the relative position of women and men varies from society to society, gender hierarchies that privilege men and masculinity over women and femininity can be found, to different degrees, all over the world (Peterson and Runyan 1999). On a global level, women comprise more than 70 percent of the world's impoverished, face restricted educational opportunities, are politically underrepresented, and make between one-half and three-quarters the wages of their male counterparts (Neft and Levine 1997).

The structural dimension of gender, on one level, refers to the way in which it organizes social life and divides labor into separate spheres associated with women and men—e.g., in some societies, the private and public spheres, respectively. Reflecting a gendered division of labor, women and men in a society are not only assigned different roles and responsibilities, these positionings are valued differently and placed in rank order. Gender roles that accompany each status consist of realms of responsibility and sets of expectations of women and men in a society. For example, within the westernized family structure, the norm is for the woman to do the expressive work in the private realm, that is, cement relationships, provide emotional support, and nurture. Men, on the other hand, are supposed to do instrumental work by supplying resources to the family and linking it to the public sphere or work world. The fact is, though, these realms of social life are not mutually exclusive but intricately interrelated and interdependent. The public and private spheres of human activity and labor have only been conceptually distinct in recent history and western-dominated societies. In reality, both women and men perform productive/public and reproductive/private labor. Even so, individuals internalize and transmit these roles and behavioral sets through the process of gender socialization.

A gendered mode of analysis entails taking the process, stratification, and structure of gender into account when viewing social phenomena. This mode of analysis acknowledges that institutionalized gender relations and inequalities impact the human social experience in both constraining and catalytic ways. In this book, I incorporate the idea of the "dialectic," the struggle between maintaining and changing status quo gender relations as a force of change and social transformation. I also follow in the path of more recent social movement scholarship and research that has taken gendered analysis even further by assessing how systems of racial stratification and class inequality interact with gender differences in social movement processes (Brewer 1989; Collins 1990).

Social Movements through a Gender Lens

Over the last three decades, social movement scholars have made concerted efforts to gender the study of social movements (Einwohner et al. 2000; McAdam 1992; Neuhouser 1995; Taylor and Whittier 1998, 1999; West and Blumberg 1990). The initial impulse in gendering the study of social resistance was directed toward reducing the invisibility of women (Barnett 1993; Randall 1981; West and Blumberg 1990). Scholars argued that women's perspective had been ignored and the significance of their social location needed to be incorporated into the study and practice of social resistance (Eisenstein 1991; West and Blumberg 1990). Androcentrism, or male-centric bias, in social movements and the study of them had obscured the presence and devalued the role of women in those movements. As a corrective to the gender bias in social movement research, this new wave of research focused attention on women's experience within gender-integrated movements, individual women, and autonomous women's organizations within larger movements (Cantarow and O'Malley 1980; Evans 1979; Freeman 1973, 1979; Walker 1982).

This was basically the "sex role" stage of gendering social movement research. Emphasis was placed on making women visible as social movement leaders, participants, opponents and supporters. While useful descriptively, to focus solely on women limited the analysis to social categories, reinforced a dichotomous view of gender (i.e., female versus male), and ignored gender as a larger social process and institution (Hess and Ferree 1987). Further, this tendency effectively essentialized the categories of woman versus man and implied a monolithic reality within these categories. However, viewing women in social movements and social movements through the experience of women was a necessary step toward a more critical and complete understanding of social movements from a gendered perspective. It led theorists and activists to acknowledge the broader effects of gender as a system of relational inequalities and its impact on resistance and protest.

Contemporary gender-conscious social movement research is a logical continuation of these initial efforts to subvert the male bias in social movement scholarship and to increase the inclusivity and the validation of women's experience in the study of social movements (Einwohner et al. 2000; Neuhouser 1995; Noonan 1995; West and Blumberg 1990). Beyond emphasizing the role that women and women's organizations have played in social change movements, this more recent scholarship treats all social movements as "gendered processes." It explores the ways in which gender impacts all social movement emergence, development, sustenance, and decline (Sharoni 1995b; Einwohner, Hollander, and Olson 1996; Neuhouser 1995). As one researcher put it,

> Gender differences are crucial in understanding why and how women and men organize and participate in urban struggle. Women and men perform different roles, have distinct needs, social responsibilities, expectations and power, and are socialized in different ways. Gender as a social construction explains the social relations between men and women, which are dialectic and vary with class, race, culture, age, and religion. (Rodriguez 1994, 35)

The emergent gender-conscious discourse on social movements and collective action has commonly stressed the following:

1) the salience of gender as an analytical category as opposed to simply a backdrop or an add-on "variable";
2) transcendence of the "separate spheres" and dichotomous models of gender;
3) rethinking established social movement theories and frameworks, taking gendered critiques into account;
4) the interrelationship of gender with systems of race, ethnicity, class, culture, and sexuality;
5) the complex and dynamic nature of gendered processes, which both catalyze and impede social movement processes.

Through this lens, activists and movement scholars began to view social movements differently.

The gendered nature of social movements is not straightforward. On the one hand, gender roles, ideologies, and power systems can inhibit social movement activities and processes. On the other hand, these same gendered patterns can catalyze particular actions and contribute to the dynamism of social movement processes. For example, as discussed in more detail later in this volume, prescribed gender roles that placed limitations on women's political involvement in the anti-apartheid, civil rights, and Black Power movements often served as catalysts leading to the development of alternative organizational structures and strategic opportunities for resistance. The Federation of South African Women (FSAW), in which Frances Baard was involved during the early 1950s, is an example of such an organization. Its very existence was related to restrictions placed on women's roles within the African National Congress (ANC) and other movement organs.

Gender, on both objective and subjective levels, significantly impacts social movement recruitment and mobilization, roles played and activities performed within movements, resistance strategies and organizational structures, and the relevance and impact of movement outcomes. As a result, taking gendered patterns into account opens up a Pandora's box of previously unasked questions and concerns. For instance, what impact does the societal gendered division of labor have on fueling and motivating protest? To what degree were these divisions and "gender roles" reproduced or undermined during a liberation struggle? How were the experiences within movement actions differentiated by gender? Were the objectives of the movement the same when viewed through women's eyes, as opposed to men's? What about the outcomes? At every turn, these questions and their answers reveal relationships to gendered structures, ideologies, symbols, and roles. What follows are some examples of the types of questions and answers that gendered social movement studies have engendered.

Movement Emergence, Mobilization, and Recruitment

From a gender lens perspective, we might begin by asking questions about the relationships between the reasons that movements emerge and the gendered divisions that differentially encourage or impede participation in movement activities. How are gender inequalities related to the precipitants that lead people to protest and rebellion? Does gender differentiation and stratification in the society stimulate movement emergence by creating grievances that are particular to women's versus men's lives? How does structural gender inequality and stratification that places women in a subordinate position relative to men in most societies worldwide impact grievances and motivations for involvement in social resistance (Peterson and Runyan 1999; Seager 1997)? Further, the gendered nature of social institutions like the economy, workforce, and political system may offer different opportunities for and avenues toward movement mobilization.

On a mesolevel, social movements are also characterized by gender differentiated recruitment processes and organizational structures. In his research on the civil rights movement, McAdam (1992) discovered that gender was significantly related to whether applicants would be accepted for participation in the 1964 Freedom Summer project. In the selection of northern (most by European American/White) college students to assist the

Student Nonviolent Coordinating Committee (SNCC) in registering African American voters in Mississippi, issues related to sexuality and physical appearance that were used to evaluate female applicants were not applied to their male counterparts, for example.

Micromobilization refers to the individual level processes involved in drawing people to join and participate in movement efforts (Klandermans 1984, 1986). What about the mobilization paths or avenues by which individuals get involved in movements? Are they different for women and men? According to scholars like Lila Rodriguez (1994), they are. She found a female bias toward entering movements through residence-based political struggles that were grounded in the community and focused on immediate needs (e.g., housing and related services, child care, and transportation needs). This contrasted with the more male-dominated production struggles in the workplace and political realm (Kaplan 1990; Rodriguez 1994). Rodriguez (1994) concluded that gendered divisions of labor that placed disproportionate domestic and childrearing responsibilities on women make them more dependent on and integrated in community and kinship networks than men.

Similarly, Sherry Cable (1992) found in her study of an environmental protest organization in Kentucky that gender distinctions in domestic and childrearing responsibilities made women and men differentially available to participate in social protest. She described this gendered pattern as unequal levels of "structural availability" (Cable 1992). On the other hand, "traditional gender roles and family obligations may actually spur women to participate in movements that are not consciously about gender" (Neuhouser 1995, 95). The constraints and responsibilities associated with the family and community work may create particular needs and interests in transforming social conditions.

Organizational Structures and Movement Roles: Gendered Divisions of Movement Labor

Even the way in which movement organizations are structured reflects gender distinctions and hierarchies. In many liberation movements, men are associated with the movement's formal structures, such as trade unions and political parties, while women are more likely to ease into political action through community and neighborhood groupings and informal kinship networks (Kaplan 1990; Robnett 1997; Rodriguez 1994). In the resistance communities of Brazil, for example, "women were less likely than men to create formal organizational structures, relying instead on informal social exchange networks" (Neuhouser 1995, 40). West and Blumberg (1990) identify three patterns in "the continuum of gender integration in social protest: independent, gender-integrated, and gender-parallel." Gender-independent movements and/or groups are those in which the genders are separate and operate autonomously both structurally and ideologically. Women's movements that are focused on gender equality and/or other gender issues are examples of this place on the continuum. In contrast, gender-integrated movements and organizations engage both women and men pursuing a single objective which is usually not gender related such as national liberation or racial equity. Gender-parallel structures are auxiliary groups which usually link women and their separate structures to a single or set of male-dominated movement organizations with some mutually beneficial movement objective. Much of the contemporary scholarship is concerned with identifying gendered patterns within the gender-integrated and gender-parallel movements.

Research on gender-integrated movements has identified complex patterns of labor and leadership divisions within movements. In some cases, these divisions seem to mirror the relegation of women and men to private and public spheres, respectively. This is especially noticeable in liberation movements that utilize guerrilla warfare. With notable exceptions, these movements are often characterized by men on the "front lines" as "freedom fighters" and women in the background in positions of support (Lobao 1990). This gender asymmetry and male dominance in movement organizational hierarchies has been viewed as a movement catalyst as well. The female presence at the grassroots and bridging level of the struggle where there are "free spaces" is a movement resource (Robnett 1997; Rodriguez 1994).

A gendered analysis forces us to look below the surface of these dichotomized movement roles and to not assume that these gendered patterns are simplistic reflections of differential value or contribution to movement efforts. A view through a gender lens forces us to reconceptualize the idea of leadership in a way that equally values the power and importance of a variety of movement roles. In this spirit, the movement role of cementing relationships between the movement masses and the organizations or linking organizations to each other is valued as a leadership role, despite the absence of an official title. Scholars have reassessed the role of the women who were active in the more hidden crevices and "open spaces" of social movements, such as in the civil rights and anti-apartheid movements. They are "invisible leaders" according to Bernice

McNair Barnett (1995), "bridge leaders" in Belinda Robnett's (1997) analysis, and "centerwomen" as defined by Karen Sachs (1988). This tier of movement is not in the forefront but is crucial to movement sustenance since it links movement organizations to the grassroots level. Activists Ella Baker and Frances Baard were quintessential bridge leaders: They organized from below, linked movement organizations to each other, and galvanized mass support. Unfortunately, this tier of participation in most movements also remains in relative obscurity.

Social movements are also sites for contestation against normative gendered divisions of labor and social roles. The typical arrangement in guerrilla warfare in which men predominate as armed resistance fighters while women maintain the home front was challenged in the 1970s during the Nicaraguan movement to establish a socialist government led by the Sandinista National Liberation Front (FSLN). By 1979, close to thirty percent of the FSLN guerrilla fighters were women (Lobao 1990). This distribution clearly counters the traditional notions of femininity and masculinity.

Scholarly attention has also been paid to the dynamic and shifting nature of gender divisions of movement labor. While many grassroots protests are women led initially, the leadership is more likely to become male dominated as the movement becomes institutionalized (Lawson and Barton 1980). In their study of the tenant's rights movement in New York City, Ronald Lawson and Stephen E. Barton (1980) found sex role patterns in which women were the earliest organizers of protests in their buildings but were later replaced by male leadership.

Gendered Collective Action Frames and Identities

What about the subjective level? How do movement ideologies and symbol systems reflect and transform gender? A gendered perspective can be used to highlight the ways in which gender ideologies and identities are embedded in the framing and identity construction processes of social movements. Symbols and meaning systems that involve gender are often incorporated into the logic of the resistance movements and utilized strategically during the course of a movement. Some national liberation movements have, for example, used gendered analogies to depict their struggle. In the Palestinian movement, activists likened the colonized land to a raped and/or violated woman in need of patriarchal or male protection or vengeance (Sharoni 1995b). In these ways, gendered symbols, identities, and images have been deployed, strategically, to achieve movement objectives.

The "maternal frame," which centers women's activism in "the language and cultural themes of mothering and appropriate activities for women," is a case in point (Noonan 1995, 92). Some of the most well-known instances of the "maternal frame" were in Chile, Argentina, El Salvador, and Guatemala during the 1970s and 1980s. Groups such as *Co-Madres* in El Salvador, *Madres de la Plaza de Mayo* in Argentina, and *Grupo Apoyo Mutuo* (GAM) in Guatemala demanded information from the government about the disappearances of their loved ones on the basis of their identities as mothers and wives (Agosin 1990). Because of the patriarchal attitudes of the repressive nation-states, the status of "mother" also protected these women from the extreme violent repression that was prevalent against dissidents in those countries at the time. Likewise, in South Africa women linked their protest activities to their work as mothers to create stable family lives for their children. During the anti-pass campaign of the 1950s, the Federation of South African Women capitalized on the prescribed collective identity as "mother" shared by women to justify their involvement in the anti-apartheid and national liberation movement (Walker 1982; Wells 1993). Ironically, this same identity would be later used by the male-led faction of the movement as a rationale for women to reduce their activism.

Traditional gender frames and identities have been drawn on for different purposes and to facilitate divergent political interests (Noonan 1995; Ginsburg 1991). Critics of using the "motherist frame" in social resistance charge that it utilizes dichotomous notions of women's and men's roles, and therefore limit the cultural frames of resistance available to movement participants. These same gender constructs can then be constraints on women's full social movement participation and gender transformations following successful social change movements (Lobao 1990; Mies 1986). The social construction, deconstruction, and deployment of gender identities plays a role in resistance and social movements for change.

Outcomes and Transformations

Do all participants or society members experience social movement results and outcomes in the same way? How do social movements reinforce or transform established gender relations and norms? Maxine

Molyneux (1985) theorizes the existence of differential "gender interests," that is, the different stakes that women and men have in particular social changes by virtue of their social positioning. She differentiates between "strategic gender interests," which are concerned with more broad-based and long-term issues of gender equality, and "practical gender interests," those grounded in more immediate, short-term needs.

Social movements are also sites for "gendering consciousness" (Craske 1993). This idea is related to Judith Lorber's discussion of "doing gender," that is, the process through which gender meanings, roles, relations, and identities are continually being constructed and revised. Social resistance often fosters an awareness of gender roles and relations even when the target and ultimate objectives of the movement have nothing to do with gender equity. For example, both Rodriguez (1994) and Neuhouser (1995) noted the development of a gender identity that transformed further into a feminist identity among women in the community struggles in Brazil's barrios. Gender ideologies and relations were altered during the course of the movement as the women were politicized and began to see their interests as *women* as an outcome of their movement involvement.

> In the process of participation barrio women's daily lives have been affected. We have seen how the constraints of being housewives, mothers and daughters become potential forces for transforming their subordination, how gender identity emerges from collective participation, how powerless women are changing everyday power relations and politics. (Rodriguez 1994, 44)

Independent movements for gender equality and women's liberation often incubate in mixed-gender movements as a result of the increased awareness of sexism and patriarchy (Evans 1979). According to numerous scholars and activists, the U.S. women's movement of the 1970s had its birth in the gender encounters and gendering consciousness experienced by women in the civil rights, student, antiwar, and new left movements of the 1960s.

Gender ideologies in the wider society can also affect movement outcomes. Rachel Einwohner (1999) found that the legitimacy of activists' claims is often judged externally on the basis of gendered assumptions and perceptions. She compared two animal rights campaigns and found that the gender of the activists, in these cases mostly women, shaped the way that opponents received their claims. Hunters discredited and trivialized the claims of antihunting activists by arguing that they were based on emotion and sentimentality. These "feminine" characteristics were contrasted with the rationality and reason that allegedly informed the hunters' actions.

On the other hand, the linkage between perceptions of women as nurturers legitimized their claims in the case of a movement to stop cruelty to circus animals.

Social movement outcomes are gendered on both objective and subjective levels. The types of structural transformations that result from movement efforts can differentially affect women and men in terms of their relative gender interests. On the subjective level, the gendering of consciousness is a social movement outcome that can impact tensions and struggles in movements and the wider society around the roles that women and men play in society. These gender struggles catalyze the emergence of new strategies and forms of resistance, reconstruct gendered hierarchies and asymmetries, and can have a transformative effect on society at large. As we'll see in the case studies, these effects continue to be felt.

Transforming the Sociology of Social Movements

Let's return to our initial illustration of activists Ella Baker and Frances Baard. It is no coincidence that, with the exception of the women's liberation movement, most icons commonly associated with struggles for social change are men (e.g., Martin Luther King Jr. of the U.S. civil rights movement and Nelson Mandela of the South African anti-apartheid movement). This tendency reflects the fact that gendered processes, stratification, and structure exist even in movements that are not specifically concerned with gender equality or women's rights. Social movements are themselves microcosms of the types of gender processes, stratification, and structure evident in the wider society. They simultaneously embody, employ, confront, and transform how women and men are positioned, as well as perceived, within a society.

Filtering social movements through a "gender lens" has the potential of broadening and deepening our understanding of resistance activities. Use of this lens allows activities and individuals who have historically been ignored or devalued by social movement scholars, like Frances Baard and Ella Baker, to be placed more squarely within the analysis of social movements. It also demands an expanded, gendered approach to social movement activity that allows the Chilean embroidered arpilleras (Moya-Raggio 1984), Palestinian sewing collectives (Gluck 1995), South African home beer brewing (Walker 1982), and African American citizen schools to be appreciated as resistance activity on a par with participation in guerrilla warfare, unions, or political parties.

Social resistance movements can be considered gendered terrains of struggle and transformation, one of the many social landscapes on which gendered relations are negotiated. The image of "terrain" is evocative of an interactive environment that is simultaneously accommodating and harsh, inviting and dangerous. Gender, in its manifestations both internal and external to social movements, provides opportunities as well as constraints, serves as both impetus and barrier, to the social movement process.

CHAPTER 2

Background and History:
The Case Studies in Comparative Gender
Perspective

Prologue

On Thursday, October 27, 1955, a contingent of more than two thousand women marched on the Union Buildings in Pretoria, the capital of South Africa. Spearheaded by the Federation of South African Women (FSAW), these women came to protest the extension of pass books which would further restrict their freedom of movement and right to live in areas of their choice. With babies on their backs, from hundreds of miles away, and in defiance of governmental measures prohibiting public demonstrations, this mass of women gathered at the nation's capitol buildings and protested in silence. Due to government restrictions that kept them from making their demands verbally, the protesters left thousands of signed statements denouncing governmental intentions to require African women to carry passes on the doorsteps of the Union buildings.

The next year, on August 9, 1956, more than 20,000 women returned to the capitol building in Pretoria to make this same demand of the South African government. Despite the fact that their efforts failed to block the extension of pass laws to women, the anti-pass campaign catalyzed a new phase of the anti-apartheid struggle. To commemorate the significance of these actions, August 9 would hereafter be known as "Women's Day" in South Africa.

In December of 1955, women of African descent on the other side of the globe mobilized around a similar, but different, injustice. The Women's Political Council (WPC) in Montgomery, Alabama, spearheaded a boycott of the city bus system on the basis of its racial segregationist policies.

Twenty-four hours after Rosa Parks' historic refusal to relinquish her bus seat to a White man, the Women's Political Council (WPC) copied and distributed thousands of leaflets throughout the city calling for a one-day bus boycott. For over 380 days, more than 45,000 women, men, and children of African descent carpooled, taxied, or walked to their destinations. What began as a single-day boycott lasted more than a year and ultimately forced the Montgomery City Bus Lines to integrate seating on the bus system.

In both of these campaigns, gender, along with race, ethnicity, and class, was central to the mobilization of people and coordination of efforts against the legitimized power structure. The campaigns, initially led by women and their organizations, provided impetus to the male-led "official" national liberation organizations' attacks on the U.S. and South African systems of racial injustice and segregation. The grassroots mobilizations that women initiated and sustained that became known as the civil rights and anti-apartheid movements, respectively, are now popularly remembered as being male-led and organized.

This chapter provides historical background on the U.S. civil rights, Black Power, and South African anti-apartheid movements from which examples will be drawn throughout the book. I overview the sociohistorical context for these movements, chart their development, and present information on the major movement organizations, campaigns, and participants. These movements included the active participation of women and men, but often in gender-differentiated manners. The similarities and differences in these cases illustrate gendered social movement dynamics.

"Why These Movements?"
Background and Historical Context

Scholars and activists have frequently used the United States and South Africa as sites for cross-cultural comparison, especially in terms of their systems of racial and ethnic stratification (Cell 1982; Fredrickson 1981, 1995); the experiences of women as activists and movement participants (Kuumba and Alston-Dosunmu 1995; Steady 1981; Terborg-Penn 1990); and the philosophies and strategies of the social movements that emerged in both societies (Fredrickson 1998; Terborg-Penn 1990). While these societies differ in their racial/ethnic composition and many other specific characteristics, their system of racial domination, intersected with gender stratification, and active mass movements for racial equality and national liberation serve as the basis for this comparative analysis.

Tripartite Systems of Racial Domination

The race, class, and gender stratified systems in the United States and South Africa developed as outgrowths of sixteenth-century European colonialism and capitalist expansion. Through the colonial penetration of Africa, European powers and budding capitalist entities were able to secure land and natural resources, cheap labor, and consumer markets favorable to their interests. The colonial incursion of the Dutch into South Africa in 1652 led to the dispossession of Africans from their traditional lands and their forced incorporation into the mining, agrarian, and service wage labor system (Magubane 1979; Fredrickson 1981; Walker 1982). The European invasion of the Americas in the early 1600s that encroached on the lands of the Native Americans brought enslaved Africans to the Western Hemisphere as forced laborers in a plantation system and agrarian economy.

While the United States and South Africa became multiethnic societies, they developed bipolar (black/white) conceptions and constructions of race relations, with people of African descent at the lowest socioeconomic realms. By the mid-nineteenth century, people of African descent in both the United States and South African societies found themselves in a subjugated position, either as directly or "internally" colonized. As a precipitant to the emergence of the civil rights and anti-apartheid movements, people of African descent suffered under a "tripartite" system of racial domination characterized by (1) economic exploitation, (2) political subjugation and disenfranchisement, and (3) social oppression and segregation (Morris 1984).

Economic Exploitation

The exploitation of cheap and unpaid African labor served as a basis for capital accumulation and industrial growth in both the U.S. and South African societies. Before the emergence of the civil rights movement in the United States, people of African descent in both societies mainly served as cheap, unskilled labor and experienced high rates of economic marginality and depression. This process was institutionalized as a split labor market in which workers of African descent were excluded from specific occupations or received differential wages for doing the same work as their European American counterparts (Bonacich 1987).

As Aldon Morris related in his landmark study of the civil rights movement, African Americans in the U.S. South occupied the lowest realms of a racially split labor market.

> In a typical Southern city during the 1950s at least 75 percent of the black men in the labor force were employed in unskilled jobs. They were the janitors, porters, cooks, machine operators, and common laborers. (Morris 1984, 1)

African American women were exploited in the labor market in different capacities, serving primarily as domestic servants.

As a result of this labor market stratification, African Americans occupied the lowest economic levels. In 1950, the African American family only earned 54 percent of the median income of their European American counterparts (Morris 1984). Unemployment and poverty were rampant in the African American community.

In South Africa at this same time, Africans were economically exploited and at the lowest socioeconomic levels relative to the other three major "racial" groups in South Africa: Europeans/Whites, Coloureds, and Indians. The indigenous Africans were dispossessed of their land as a result of European incursion and consequently lost the ability to sustain themselves. The Nationalist Party, which took power in South Africa in 1948, further institutionalized White supremacy and established the system of racial domination and separation called "apartheid." Apartheid, literally translated as "separateness" in Afrikaans, interlocked racist legislation and institutional processes that facilitated tripartite racial domination and White supremacy.

The Land Acts of 1913, 1936, and 1963 relegated "legal" African residence to "native reserves" which accounted for approximately 13 percent of the land in the country. The absence of income-generating opportunities on the overcrowded reserves facilitated the development of a migratory labor system in which mostly males of African descent traveled to the White farms, urban areas, or mines to find work. During the 1950s, labor laws restricted Africans to the unskilled jobs. In order to protect the working class White/Afrikaner population, wage limitations were placed on African workers (Seidman 1994). African workers were also forced to carry identification books, more commonly known as "passes," to verify their employment, their only legitimate reason for being in White-dominated urban areas. Laws like the Urban Areas Act, Population Registration Act, and the Groups Areas Act restricted African residence and authorized their forced removal of "redundant natives"—that is, those Africans in excess of the labor needs of the area (Hindson 1987). This system of "influx" regulated the employment, residence, and movement of Africans in the interests of the White industry owners, farmers, and workers (Magubane 1979).

As a result of Jim Crow and apartheid laws and practices, the African populations in both the United States and South Africa were economically exploited and oppressed. As discussed more later, these economic hardships were experienced differently by women and men.

Political Subjugation and Disenfranchisement

People of African descent were systematically denied the right to vote and denied input into the legitimate political process in both the United States and South Africa. Formal and informal measures were used to restrict people of African descent in both countries from political participation and representation.

In the United States during the 1950s and 1960s, various repressive and restrictive strategies were used to keep African Americans in the South from registering to vote, despite their legal right to do so. These included:

> requiring one or more white character witnesses; requiring only Black applicants to show property tax receipts; strict enforcement of literacy tests against Negro applicants; rejecting Black applicants because of technical mistakes in filling out registration forms or requiring Black applicants to fill out their own forms while those of whites were filled out by registration officials; a variety of evasive tactics, such as claiming that registration board members had to be present, or that it was closing time; putting difficult questions about the Constitution to Negro applicants; holding registration in private homes, which Blacks were reluctant to enter. (Payne 1995, 26)

As a result of these actions, people of African descent were unable to exercise their political rights or gain political representation.

In South Africa, the restrictions that Africans faced in residence and land ownership also impacted their right to vote and be politically represented. The Bantu Authority Act of 1951 established a system of indirect rule in which African chiefs, hand picked by the South African government, became the political representatives of Africans assigned to particular homelands. On the basis of the tribal authorities, Africans were excluded from the South African Parliament. Since Africans could not "legally" or permanently reside in South Africa's urban areas they were officially excluded from the political processes as well.

In both the U.S. and South African cases, people of African descent were systematically excluded from the legitimate decision-making processes. They were not allowed to vote, restricted from holding political office, and, effectively, "internally colonized" and ruled by the dominant European/ White society.

Social Oppression: Racial Residential Segregation and Discrimination

The third component of the tripartite system of racial domination, according to Aldon Morris, is the denial of personal freedoms to people of African descent (Morris 1984). This type of social oppression included racial residential segregation, physical separation, and other forms of discrimination experienced by people of African descent. Racial residential segregation and social discrimination were "petty apartheid" processes that existed in both the United States and South Africa during the 1950s and contributed to the emergence of mass movements.

The Jim Crow system of rigid racial segregation in all areas of social life was dominant in the U.S. South during the 1950s. This culture of "Jim Crow" institutionalized the "separate but equal" doctrine that the *Plessy v Fergusen* decision of 1886 upheld. Later found unconstitutional by the *Brown v Topeka Board of Education* decision in 1954, the practice of racial segregation and inequality in all areas of social life (e.g., education, medical care, and residence) persisted into the 1960s.

Not only were people of African descent forced to live separately, they were prescribed separate public facilities and social institutions. The areas in which they were designated to live were consistently the most underdeveloped, overcrowded, and lacking of social services. The resources provided for education and schools were inferior in comparison to those in the European American (White) communities. In addition, health facilities in African American communities were also pitifully substandard, resulting in higher infant mortality and lower life expectancy rates. In addition, the racist ideology that justified these practices often fueled hostilities that led to harassment by European American citizens, organizations, and police. These processes combined to take both psychological and physical tolls on African Americans. As already indicated, spatial segregation by race was a central component of the South African apartheid and migratory labor system. In addition to the system of territorial segregation that relegated Africans to particular homelands or "native reserves" as a result of the Land Acts, the Urban Areas Act of 1923 and the Bantu

Authorities Act of 1951 limited Africans' rights to reside in the urban areas. Legally banned from urban area residence, except those male laborers with employment and a valid "pass," African migrants established townships and "shantytowns" like Soweto and Crossroads at the edges of cities like Johannesburg and Capetown. These areas were often characterized by extreme poverty and lacked even basic amenities like running water and electricity. The legalized segregation and "reservationizing" of Africans in South Africa had an impact on their access to other social services and necessities, e.g., education, health care, and transportation. Completing the vicious cycle, the Bantu Education Act of 1953 brought African education under the Department of Native Affairs and imposed an inferior system geared to prepare Africans for unskilled labor (Walker 1982).

As a result of the tripartite system of racial domination, Africans were placed at the bottom of both the U.S. and South African racial-class hierarchy. Institutionalized processes and continued discrimination have maintained this racialized stratification system into the present.

Multiplying Oppressions:
Gender Intersecting Race-Class Domination

Racial domination and class inequality on the economic, political, and social/personal levels was accompanied by gender stratification, as colonial domination often builds on and intensifies already existing sexual divisions and indigenous patriarchies (Boserup 1970; Seidman 1993). In both U.S. and South African society, women of African descent experienced multiplicative or simultaneous oppressions from at least three sources—racism, classism, and sexism (King 1988; Collins 1990).

In the 1950s, African American women experienced this threefold oppression in the home and African American community, the workforce, and the larger society. While sharing race-class inequality with their male counterparts in their cities and in the labor market, African American women faced additional constraints and burdens on the basis of their disproportionate family and community responsibilities (Giddings 1984). African American women were forced by economic necessity to work outside the home. During this period, more than 50 percent of African American women workers were domestic servants in White households (Aulette and Katz Fishman 1991; Morris 1984). In addition to being forced into these lower status and lower wage occupations, African American women were also subject to sexual advances and assaults by their male employers in the European American households in which they labored (Davis 1981). They coupled their worklife with disproportionate responsibility for rearing children and maintaining their own households.

In South Africa during this same period, the apartheid system differentially affected women and men. The migratory labor system, structured to attract cheap African male labor to the mines and urban areas, severely limited the movement of women. Even wives of the male workers were kept from moving to the urban or "White" areas (Walker 1982; Wells 1993). African female labor was directed toward social reproduction and subsistence farming in the "native reserves" (Magubane 1979; Walker 1982). And,

> in the process, the social division of labour between the sexes took on an added geographical dimension—the men in the towns (and on the farms), the women in the reserves (and on the farms). The men engaged in waged labour, the women engaged in unwaged productive and reproductive labour. And it is this geographical division which became essential to the perpetuation of colonial relations in changing conditions. (Marcus 1988, 97)

The unpaid social reproductive labor of African women subsidized the South African economy by facilitating the existence of an underpaid urban male labor force (Marcus 1988; Seidman 1993).

Despite the intentions by the government to keep African women from residing in or around urban areas, they migrated from the depressed rural areas in search of employment opportunities and freedom from patriarchal cultural norms. Beginning in the 1930s, large numbers of African women migrated to the urban areas and were forced to erect squatter's camps along the margins of the urban areas (Cole 1987; Wells 1993). When African women did enter the urban and industrial labor force, their occupational distribution was directed by embedded patriarchal gender norms (Walker 1982; Wells 1993). The majority of African women worked as domestic servants, but many also found jobs in the textile, clothing, and canning industries or earned income in the informal or underground economy as street vendors and beer brewers (Vukani Makhosikazi Collective 1985). These occupations, taken together with the restrictions placed on women's legal work and residence, made them more vulnerable to arrests and deportations (Vukani Makhosikazi Collective 1985). Gender differentiation was also evident within African societies. Customary laws and traditional South African cultural practices placed specific limitations on the women's roles and range of activities. These cultural prescriptions classified women as perpetual minors under the charge of either father, husband, or eldest son.

Thus, women of African descent in the United States and South Africa were subject not only to the tripartite system of racial domination, but also to the combined patriarchies of the Jim Crow/apartheid regimes, capitalist industrial relations, and indigenous African customary law and/or family practices. In both societies, gender intersected racial and class inequalities to systematically disadvantage women and men of African descent in profound, yet different, ways.

The civil rights, Black Power, and anti-apartheid movements reflected and transformed this gender/race/class nexus. While these movements were primarily concerned with confronting and changing systems of oppression on the basis of race, ethnicity, and national origin, they were also gendered on many levels. These movements embodied and confronted the "multiple and simultaneous oppression" experienced by women of African descent.

Gender Integration and Parallelism in Social Movements

In terms of West and Blumberg's (1990) continuum of patterns of gendered movements, the civil rights, Black Power, and anti-apartheid movements can be described as gender-integrated and gender-parallel. Gender-parallel movements include both women and men in the same movement but in separate structures and activities. Full gender-integration movements engage women and men in overlapping movement structures and tasks to achieve common goals. On the opposite side of the continuum are gender-independent movements in which women and men are involved in completely separate actions and organizations with different projects and ultimate objectives.

The civil rights, Black Power, and anti-apartheid movements went through phases of gender integration and parallelism. Overall, these movements and their official structures were highly gender-integrated, characterized by high levels of involvement by both women and men as participants or "rank and file" members. Very often, though, women and men played different roles and distinct statuses within these movements and their organizations. At times, the movements worked through gender-parallel or separated structures and processes that contributed to the same activities or ultimate objectives (Barnett 1993; Walker 1982; Wells 1993; West and Blumberg 1990). Male-led organizations became visibly associated with each movement, while women's networks and organizations played key but less visible roles as change agents in both movements. These gendered patterns were manifest differently within each movement and in distinct movement eras.

Civil Rights and Black Power in the United States

The modern phase of the U.S. civil rights era is often traced back to the Montgomery, Alabama, bus boycott of 1955. One year after *Brown v Topeka Board of Education* ruled the "separate but equal" doctrine unconstitutional, this successful year-long boycott of the city bus lines changed the Jim Crow seating practices of racial segregation and established an integrated seating system based on "first come, first served." This economic boycott was predated by a similar bus boycott in Baton Rouge, Louisiana, two years earlier. Until the mid-1960s, nonviolent direct action strategies like boycotts, sit-ins, and demonstrations were the main form of protest against racial segregation and discrimination. Campaigns used direct action, employing "a battery of acts and techniques designed to cause disruption" (Morris 1984, 50). Some of the most popularized and best remembered actions include: the Montgomery Bus Boycott; anti-segregation sit-ins catalyzed by students in Greensboro, North Carolina, in 1960; the Freedom Rides through southern states to test compliance with bus desegregation orders; voter registration drives of Freedom Summer in 1964; and the Mississippi Freedom Democratic Party campaign (McAdam 1992; Payne 1995; Robinson 1987; Zinn 1964).

Between 1966 and 1974, the racial liberation movement in the United States moved into what some have termed the "Black Power" or "masculine decade" (Giddings 1984; Robnett 1996, 1997). Internally, SNCC and CORE decided to expel Whites from the organizations, thus creating greater racial polarization in the movement (Fleming 1998; Meier and Rudwick 1973). The call to "Black Power" was first made publicly in 1966 at a march through Mississippi that was countered by White violence and resistance. From the Black Power viewpoint, the African American community, exploited and dominated by a White capitalist power structure, had to unify internally to achieve equal rights.

This phase contrasted with the nonviolent, civil disobedience–type tactics and integrationist objectives of the earlier phase of the NLM. These changes also coincided with a regional shift from the rural South to "the urban north as a locus of protest activity" (McAdam 1997, 349). Organizations like the Black Panther Party for Self-Defense (BPP) and the Republic of New Africa (RNA), formed in 1966 and 1968 respectively, grew rapidly in major U.S. cities in the late 1960s and early 1970s. Their confrontational approach marked a visible shift in the civil rights movement to include self-defense and "Black Power."

In the following discussion, I overview three major campaigns in, and the gendered patterns of, these movement eras. The Montgomery Bus Boycott, Freedom Summer, and the rise of the Black Panther Party figured prominently in movement developments.

The Montgomery Bus Boycott and Gender Parallelism

Most people who are familiar with U.S. history know the story of Rosa Parks, the African American seamstress who refused to relinquish her seat on the Montgomery City Bus Lines to a White man on December 1, 1955. Her subsequent arrest precipitated the thirteen-month boycott that resulted in a federal court ruling that declared racially segregated seating on city buses unconstitutional and in violation of the U.S. Constitution's guarantee of equal treatment by the government for citizens. Despite harassment, grand jury investigation, and arrests intended to undermine the campaign, the city was forced to adopt a desegregated seating policy five months after the federal court ruling. One of the first passengers to take advantage of the desegregated seating policy was Rosa Parks. There are some important aspects of the Montgomery Bus Boycott that are less well known, however. Rosa Parks is usually portrayed as a domestic worker whose sole motivation for remaining in her seat was her weariness. This portrayal "jives" nicely with our stereotypical images of women as passive and emotionally driven. What usually goes underacknowledged is Rosa Parks' long history of involvement in civil rights organizations; not only was she an officer with the local branch of the National Association for the Advancement of Colored People (NAACP), she had returned from civil rights workshops led by Septima Clark at the Highlander Folk School in Monteagle, Tennessee, just prior to her resistance to segregation on the bus lines (Robnett 1997).

African American women constituted a majority of the boycotters and were central to the initiation, sustenance, and ultimate success of the boycott. Employed primarily as domestic servants in the households of middle- and upper-class European Americans, many African American women had to travel across town daily on public transportation. In addition, if an African American household had a car, the male was more likely to control it. These gendered realities led the Women's Political Council (WPC), a "black professional women's civic group" formed in 1946 with the purpose of improving the status of African Americans, to contemplate a bus boycott.

Even prior to Rosa Parks' action, the WPC had been discussing and planning for a boycott of the Montgomery City Bus Lines (Robinson 1987). They had, in fact, already met with the bus company officials to protest increasing bus fares and press the city lines into more humane treatment of African American customers. According to Jo Ann Gibson Robinson, president of the WPC in 1955:

> The question of boycotting came up again and loomed in the minds of thousands of black people. We could see that black people—men, women, and children—were tired. . . . The women felt not that their cup of tolerance was overflowing, but that it had overflowed; they simply could not take anymore. They were ready to boycott. On paper, the WPC had already planned for fifty thousand notices calling people to boycott the buses; only the specifics of time and place had to be added. (Robinson 1987, 39)

Under Robinson's leadership, the WPC proceeded with boycott preparations and enlisted the support of key institutions within the African American community, not the least of which were the churches. The congregations of the churches, mostly women, pressed the ministers to support the boycott. At a mass meeting at Holt Street Church on the evening of December 5, 1955, the Montgomery Improvement Association (MIA) was formed as a coordinating body for the boycott. Dr. Martin Luther King, the young, recently appointed minister of Dexter Avenue Baptist Church, was voted president of a predominantly male executive board. The Montgomery Improvement Association (MIA) raised funds for the boycott and coordinated transportation for the mostly female domestic workforce to the White areas. The organization was assisted, though, by two women's organizations—"The Club from Nowhere" and "The Friendly Club"—which competed with each other in raising funds.

This early phase of the movement has been noted for its gender integration, despite the existence of different, but equally important, spheres of leadership occupied by women and men. The male-led movement superstructure, which consisted of official movement organizations, was only effective because of its majority female constituency and autonomous women's organizations like the WPC, the Club from Nowhere, and the Friendly Club (Barnett 1993; Payne 1990; Robnett 1996, 1997). The informal community and church networks that women controlled were also crucial support for the efforts of the movement. This gender-parallelism served as an adaptation to maneuver around the gender constraints and hierarchies in the main movement organs. This configuration allowed for interaction within and between movement structures and for the wide but differentiated inclusion of both women and men. It also created gender struggles that, in fact, acted as important movement catalysts.

Freedom High: SNCC, Freedom Summer,
and the Mississippi Freedom Democratic Party

The Southern Christian Leadership Conference (SCLC), a coalition of southern ministers, also emerged from the Montgomery Bus Boycott, and Ella Baker served as its first executive secretary. By this time Baker was an already seasoned activist who could draw from her work with the Young Negroes' Cooperative League in Harlem, New York, during the 1930s which she co-founded and as a field secretary for the National Association for the Advancement of Colored People (NAACP) during the 1940s. These experiences had provided Baker with a highly developed political consciousness, a wealth of contacts with organizers in the North and the South, and extensive organizing expertise (Cantarow and O'Malley 1980; Grant 1998; James 1994).

Ella Baker and other SCLC founders viewed the organization as a potential vehicle for organizing a mass movement. However, it was handicapped by its hierarchical structure and the conservative gradualistic approach of the male ministerial leadership. According to biographer Joanne Grant, Baker "was exasperated by the failure of SCLC to function as a 'group-centered leadership, rather than a leadership-centered group'" (Grant 1998, 123). By that time, Baker had become closely associated with the Citizenship Education Program of the Highlander Folk School, which was more inclined toward mass education and action. Directed by Septima Clark, an African American public school teacher who had lost her job for not denouncing her NAACP membership, Highlander focused on adult education geared toward political awareness and voter registration in the South. Aldon Morris referred to entities like the Highlander Folk School as "movement halfway houses," organizations geared toward changing the dominant society within which they are partially integrated (Morris 1984). Ella Baker's political vision was more aligned with the strategy of mass organizing potential that the Highlander program facilitated, than with SCLC's elitist approach.

The wave of sit-ins that spread across the South after four college students challenged the segregationist policies of a Woolworth's lunch counter in Greensboro, North Carolina, in 1960 was inspiring to Baker. Within weeks, sit-ins had spread throughout the South. In an effort to feed the momentum created by these actions, Baker called a meeting of the young activists for Easter weekend of 1960 at Shaw University in Raleigh, North Carolina. This meeting gave birth to the Student Nonviolent Coordinating Committee (SNCC), the organization that would usher in the next phase of the civil rights movement.

After its inaugural weekend, SNCC established itself as a permanent organization with Ella Baker as one of its first staff members. Over the next six years, SNCC coordinated a variety of campaigns in the South to challenge the tripartite system of racial domination. Many of the SNCC members such as Diane Nash and Ruby Doris Smith Robinson were involved in the Freedom Rides of 1961, a campaign of integrated bus trips through the South initiated by the Congress of Racial Equality (CORE) to press toward desegregation of interstate bus travel.

In addition to the direct action campaigns, SNCC was heavily involved in the project of getting African Americans in the South to register to vote. In 1962, SNCC received government funding for the Voter Education Project (VEP) and embarked on an expanded drive to register Black voters. The White power structure and resistant White citizens responded to SNCC efforts with violence, harassment, arrests, and killings. Despite this repression, SNCC maintained and even increased its voter registration activities. The project reached a peak in the summer of 1964, Freedom Summer, when hundreds of northern college students, of both African and European American descent, were recruited to participate in the voter registration drive.

During this same period, SNCC organizers developed an alternative to the segregated Mississippi Democratic Party that was called the Mississippi Freedom Democratic Party (MFDP). The MFDP served as a mechanism for African Americans to participate in elections. It held statewide mock elections, ran its own candidates, and elected its own state representatives. One of its first elected congresspersons was Mrs. Fannie Lou Hamer, an ex-sharecropper from Ruleville, Mississippi, who would become a leader in and a field secretary for SNCC (Payne 1995). The MFDP attempted unsuccessfully to be seated at the 1964 Democratic National Convention in Atlantic City. The MFDP delegates, although split in their positions, ultimately rejected a compromise position of two seats offered by the subcommittee of the Credentials Committee. It turns out that Fannie Lou Hamer and the other women delegates were the most staunchly against the compromise.

Because of the egalitarian philosophy, collective leadership, and decentralized governance of SNCC, women were able to exercise and develop leadership within the organization. While there were gender differentials in official leadership roles, women such as Ruby Doris Smith Robinson, Fannie Lou Hamer, and Diane Nash had a greater degree of authority and power within SNCC than other civil rights organizations. They were "bridge" or invisible leaders who played the indispensable role of linking the movement to the masses of people in the South who became participants in the movement. They made movement strategy decisions and influenced broad sectors of the movement's participants and supporters (Barnett 1993, 1995; Evans 1979; Robnett 1997).

Despite the powerful roles that many African American women played, racial and gender tensions arose within the Student Nonviolent Coordinating Committee (SNCC) that influenced the direction the organization and, ultimately, the movement took. Concerns about gender inequality and White dominance began to surface in SNCC in 1964. In that year, there was an informal women's "sit-in" by African American staffers at the SNCC offices in protest of women being relegated to the traditional female tasks such as typing and clerical roles. That same year, the now infamous position paper on "Women in the Movement" was presented anonymously at the SNCC Waveland meeting likening "male superiority" to "White superiority" (Evans 1979; Fleming 1998; Robnett 1996, 1997).

These mounting gender tensions were accompanied by a racial component. The fact that the anonymous authors of the "Women in the Movement" paper were White women was reflective of the racial differences in women's movement experiences (Evans 1979; Robnett 1997). African American women, while underrepresented in the official leadership positions, still had more autonomy and power in SNCC than their European American counterparts. There were more African American women with responsibilities as field secretaries with the ability to make decisions and engage in high-risk activism. White women were more restricted in the roles that they played because of the gendered associations embedded in the pervasive racism of the U.S. South. For "White" women to be even seen with "Black" men in the process of doing movement work in that era put everyone associated with the voter registration drives in danger (Evans 1979; Robnett 1997).

In addition, the increased numbers of European Americans who became involved in SNCC through Freedom Summer activities led to racial tensions. Conflicts arose over interracial relationships, particularly those between African American men and European American women, and the growing belief that European American participants were having disproportionate control and power in the movement. These racialized tensions reached a head at a 1966 SNCC meeting in upstate New York where Whites were voted out of the organization. Ruptures around these fault lines, in concert with disillusionment over the failure of the MFDP and of then-recent civil rights legislation, would soon emerge.

Black Power, Macho, and Mothers of the Nation

From the moment that Willie "Mukasa" Ricks and Stokely Carmichael uttered the "Black Power" cry during a 1966 march in Mississippi, the movement shifted toward a more nationalistic and radical, but, at the same time, gender-polarized course. Despite the fact that individual African American women like Fannie Lou Hamer (MFDP) and Ruby Doris Smith Robinson (SNCC) had finally achieved high leadership positions in major civil rights movement organizations, the "open spaces" for the masses of women to participate were closing.

In response to mounting frustrations and tensions around issues of race/ethnicity, gender, and nonviolence in the organization, in the SNCC elections of 1965, a more Black nationalist and less "nonviolent" faction of the organization was voted into power. This slate consisted of Stokely Carmichael, later to be known as Kwame Ture, as chairman; Ruby Doris Smith Robinson as executive secretary; and Cleveland Sellers as program secretary. Robinson was one of SNCC's core organizers and the first activists to employ the "jail, no bail" strategy as a nineteen-year-old student at Spelman College in 1961 (Fleming 1998; Zinn 1964). Despite the ascendancy of a woman to one of the highest posts in the organization, the movement trends which included strengthened hierarchy and change of organization philosophy and strategy had a negative effect on the participation of women overall.

The trends toward a more centralized approach and Northern dominated movement also took a decidedly masculinized turn with the rise of Black Power and the Black Panther Party (BPP). The Black Panther Party for Self-Defense was a militant and nationalist movement organization founded in 1966 by Huey P. Newton and Bobby Seale, two African American college students in Oakland, California. The organization grew rapidly in urban areas of the United States and is estimated to have increased to between 2,000 and 5,000 members in its first three years. The philosophy of the BPP differed from the nonviolence of the earlier civil rights movement and emphasized Black unity and liberation "by any means necessary." Its members were confrontational in both image and strategy and were identified by their distinctive black leather jackets and berets; members openly carried guns (legal in California if unloaded), directly challenged the local police, and called for more fundamental changes in the United States.

Even though an African American woman, Elaine Brown, became the chairperson of the BPP as it was declining in power, most of its official leadership was male and its image was decidedly masculine. The increased visibility of the confrontational strategies and emphasis on particular personalities reduced the emphasis on the mass actions in which women had been active in the previous movement period (Brown 1992; Giddings 1984; Robnett 1997). At the same time, a "backlash" began to brew against the leadership that women had displayed in the movement prior to 1966. As opposed to addressing gender inequality, the philosophy of Black nationalism viewed organizing around issues of gender and sexism as divisive. Many strains of the cultural nationalist philosophy, in particular, incorporated a patriarchal view that relegated women to a supportive role in the movement.

By the early 1970s, the masculinization and gender polarization within the Black Power movement would form the basis for a more gender-separated movement pattern to emerge. The rise of Black feminism, which I discuss in the final chapter, was an outgrowth of and reaction to these trends.

The Anti-Apartheid Movement in South Africa

The anti-apartheid movement had three main post-1950 phases: an early phase of mass mobilization of civil disobedience and popular resistance from 1950 to 1959; a guerrilla warfare/militaristic phase between 1960 and 1975; and a phase of community-based struggles leading up to the negotiated settlement in 1994 (Kimble and Unterhalter 1982; Taylor 1997; Walker 1982). Not only are these phases differentiated by distinct strategies, organizational structures, and elite responses, they also had different gender patterns.

The first major action in the mass mobilization phase of the anti-apartheid movement was the Defiance Campaign that began in 1952. This was initiated by the African Nationalist Congress (ANC) as part of its "Programme of Action," which called for "boycotts, strikes, civil disobedience and non-cooperation as the weapons of the future" (Davenport 1991[1977]). In Frances Baard's autobiography, she describes the campaign:

Everyone decided that we were not going to obey the laws which the government had made because if no one obeyed these laws then they would
have to take them away. So during this campaign everybody wanted to break
the laws and go to jail so that the jails would be too full of people who didn't
like the apartheid laws. (Baard 1986, 40)

During the Defiance Campaign participants were engaged in anti-pass
marches that were led by the Federation of South African Women, demonstrations against the worsening socioeconomic conditions, municipal beer
hall protests, and school and consumer boycotts (Baard 1986; Kimble and
Unterhalter 1982; Walker 1982).

This phase of the movement was characterized by gender asymmetry
in the main movement organizations. Gender norms restricted women's
roles as leaders of large movement structures such as the African National
Congress (established in 1912), the Congress of Democrats (an alliance
formed in 1953 among all of the national liberation organizations), and the
Pan-Africanist Congress (which split from the ANC in 1959). Although
women had moved out of their auxiliary member status in the ANC and
had been given voting rights in 1943 with the establishment of the ANC's
Women's League (ANCWL), they were still limited in their roles and power.
These gender restrictions provided the impetus to the formation of the Federation of South African Women (FSAW) in 1954, a semi-autonomous
multiracial organization of women.

The South African government responded to the increasing fervor of
the movement with violent repression and legislative barriers. In 1960, a
peaceful anti-pass march in the Sharpeville region of the Transvaal organized by the PAC was responded to with violence by the South African
Defense Force (SADF). More than sixty unarmed protesters were killed in
the attack (Wolpe 1990). Movement organizations and individual leaders
were banned or restricted within the country or were forced underground
or into exile. Under these conditions, many of the arenas for movement
participation closed, especially for women.

From 1960 to 1974, increased militarization characterized both the government and the movement. Born of frustration with efforts to secure
reforms through nonviolent action and the repressive governmental response, the ANC initiated guerrilla warfare and formed a military wing,
Umkhonto we Sizwe ("Spear of the Nation"), and the Pan-Africanist Congress followed suit and formed POQO, its armed force, a year later. The
shift in strategy toward guerrilla warfare which was mandated by the conditions curbed the mass character of the movement, making it the charge

of a smaller elite or vanguard and favoring the masculinized sector of the movement. Individual women continued to be active in the movement, but state repression coupled with the shift in dominance to the military sectors of the movement resulted in more gender asymmetry.

In the early 1970s, the Black Consciousness Movement (BCM) emerged among African university students. Led by Stephen Biko, this movement expressed goals of liberation from psychological, as well as material, manifestations of dominance by the White minority apartheid regime. The Black Consciousness impulse in the movement was highly influenced by the Black Power movement in the United States. While the BCM was also skewed toward a predominance of male members and leaders, many of the projects initiated by its main organization, the South African Students Organization (SASO), were community based and opened arenas for women's participation (Ramphele 1991). The broadened scope of the movement included the formation of the Black Women's Federation (BWF) in 1975. While the BWF was focused more on national than on women's liberation, it still signaled a reopening of spaces for women's political participation. One of the few female leaders in the BCM, Mamphela Ramphele, remembers that

> the thrust of the BWF reflected its aim of mobilising women as a political force in the process of liberation. . . . There is no evidence to suggest that the BWF was concerned with the special problems women experienced as a result of sexism in the private and in the public sphere. Women were important as wives, mothers, girlfriends and sisters, in fighting a common struggle against a common enemy—namely, white racism. (Ramphele 1991, 216)

These spaces would continue to open and grow in quantity and quality into the 1980s with the resurgence of community and grass roots organs, the trade unions, and the emergence of numerous other organizations, including those devoted to women and gender issues.

These conditions, catalyzed by the Soweto uprising of 1976 and the governmental reaction to it, ushered in a new movement phase. On June 16, students in this township near Johannesburg held a peaceful protest against being educated in Afrikaans, the language of the Dutch-descended "Boers." Government security forces responded to the protest, killing many unarmed children and banning additional movement organizations. This time the response on the part of the movement was quite different than it had been after the Sharpeville incident.

> Unlike what happened after Sharpeville, the repression that followed Soweto did not lead to a long period of political inactivity and apparent black resignation in the face of overwhelming white power. Soweto in fact is now recognized as a turning point in recent South African history. (Fredrickson 1995, 309)

The 1976 Soweto uprising was the spark needed to stimulate an upsurge of movement activity and increase unity among the various movement sectors (Fredrickson 1995; Kimble and Unterhalter 1982; Taylor 1997). This was followed by a time in which "the character of the mass struggle in South Africa . . . developed dramatically. It [was] a decade in which workers, youth, and women have distinguished themselves by their militancy" (Kimble and Unterhalter 1982, 30). A cross-generational, gender-inclusive, and broader movement character emerged. Unity among the various civic movements, student groups, community organizations, trade unions, and cultural/sports clubs became official with the establishment of the United Democratic Front (UDF) in 1983. The UDF accelerated the pace of movement so much that, by the end of the decade, the South African government was forced to negotiate with the liberation forces.

"You've Struck a Rock": The Women's Anti-Pass Campaign

The 1950s ushered in an increasingly higher level of activity among women. Until this time there was an absence of a mass organization among women and their political participation was haphazard and scattered (Lapchick and Urdang 1982). The Federation of South African Women (FSAW) provided a semi-autonomous outlet for women's political participation in an era of gender restrictions in the official anti-apartheid organizations. The FSAW, which was mostly African but included women from other racial/ethnic backgrounds, is credited with sparking and leading the anti-pass struggles that drove the movement forward during this period.

The organization drew its leadership from a cadre of women who gained political consciousness and organizing experience in the textile and canning trade unions during the 1930s and 1940s. Women like Frances Baard and Emma Mashinini, who would later become leaders in the movement, became union activists during this period because of a loophole in the apartheid legislation that only restricted collective bargaining among African male workers. In 1953, a small group of these women came together in an informal "meeting of women" to "focus attention on the part that women could play in the struggle for liberation" (Walker 1986, 135). This "First National Conference of Women" in 1954 brought together women from a variety of political, racial, and organizational backgrounds. In addition to the politicizing speeches and discussions of the conference, the participants elected a National Executive Committee and adopted a "Women's Charter" that laid out the objectives of the organization. This charter would be used as a basis for the Freedom Charter adopted by the Congress Alliance that spoke for the larger movement of liberation forces (see Appendix 1).

The FSAW organized branches all over the country and took up campaigns around rent increases, forced removals, and inadequate education. Its most successful campaigns were in response to the proposed extension of passes to women. The Federation initiated the anti-pass focus, and, at its height, gathered more than 20,000 women in a march to Pretoria, the government capital, in resistance to pass laws on August 9, 1956. For the next two years, the anti-pass protests and civil disobedience of the FSAW spread throughout the country and led to thousands of women being arrested and detained. In fact, this women's organization catalyzed the major campaigns of the 1950s. Kimble and Unterhalter (1982) point out that during this period "women clearly felt themselves ahead of their men in the struggle. In their report on the campaign the FSAW observed: 'Women await with impatience the active entry of men into the anti-pass campaign'" (Kimble and Unterhalter 1982, 27). National independence continued as the objective; gendered consciousness heightened as an outgrowth of contradictions that women's activism in this nationalist project created.

By 1958, masses of women in Johannesburg and Alexandra had courted arrest and refused bail. While the women of the Federation argued that the protests should continue and the jails filled to pressure the government toward change, the ANC leadership felt that they were unprepared to deal with the momentum of the movement. In Cherryl Walker's assessment, "male authority and ANC hegemony had become fused into a single issue" and were instrumental in ending the arrests and protests (Walker 1995). Although the anti-pass campaign was taken up by the larger movement, the momentum that had been generated by women dissipated. Nevertheless, the FSAW with its anti-pass campaign is an example of gender-parallelism in action. The gender restrictions within established organizations, coupled with this core of politicized women with organizing experience, stimulated the development of semi-autonomous women's organizations and wings, that organized parallel to the official movement structures. Women's organizations worked toward the same national liberation goals as the larger movement but also made demands specific to women's lives. This parallel structure and focus facilitated equivalent, but different, movement participation by women and men.

Resistance at Cato Manor and Crossroads

Two other key mass actions in the anti-apartheid movement are the protests of Cato Manor in Durban and Crossroads near Capetown.

Cato Manor was an "illegal" squatter community in Durban populated by a large number of women who had come from rural areas to be closer to the urban areas. For many of the women, the only form of economic survival was selling "home brew," a traditional beer that was viewed as more nutritious and less intoxicating than the manufactured form that was sold in municipal beer halls. Apartheid legislation outlawing the sale of home brew and encouraging patronage at municipal beer halls was an additional blow to African women's conditions. The women who brewed beer and ran establishments for people to socialize and buy brew had an intricate communication network to protect themselves from police raids and arrests. They used these networks in June of 1959 to organize an attack of more than 1,000 women on the local municipal beer hall in which they chased out customers and destroyed the "legal" beer. The government responded violently by "charg[ing] the women with batons, striking them to the ground, even hitting the babies tied to their backs" (Bernstein 1975, 96). These initial protests spread throughout Durban with an estimated 20,000 women taking part overall and provided rural women with a model for protest (Walker 1986).

Resistance against forced removals staged by women of the Crossroads Committee at Crossroads squatter's camp outside the city of Capetown in 1978, in which women blocked bulldozers from destroying their houses, illustrates a different site in the range of community resistance. Crossroads was a squatter's camp in the Cape region of South Africa which was originally established in 1975 as a temporary camp for Africans being relocated from urban to rural areas. The community residents organized a Women's Committee and a Men's Committee in response to the government's attempts to evict the residents. Although the organizations worked together in a Joint Committee, the Women's Committee was in the forefront of resistance against the removals. They made contact with outside individuals and groups like the Advice Office as early as 1975 and came together to form the "Save Crossroads" campaign when the first eviction notices were distributed (Cole 1987). Their campaign included tactics such as organizing visits of international guests, information briefings with the press, and petitions to save Crossroads. One of the most innovative strategies was the production and touring of *Imfuduso (The Exodus)*, a play developed by the Women's Committee to dramatize their experience at Crossroads. In 1979, women were voted off of the Joint Committee's decision-making body, which greatly undermined their power and input into the negotiations with the government. The more radical and resistant stance taken by the Women's Committee was eventually compromised, but its activities remained influential in the history of anti-apartheid activism.

These examples of earlier resistance played heavily into the strength of women's organizations in the latter stages of the anti-apartheid movement. A scholar at the University of Witwatersrand explains,

> During the 1980s, women played a very prominent role in organizations and in the struggles against repression. Women had by that time been considerably influenced by the experiences of women's organizations and the women's movements in many parts of the world. This had sparked a debate about the necessity of organizing as women. (Meintjes 1998, 74)

Expanded sites for movement participation provided the milieu for the incorporation of gender in the democratic transition that characterizes this latest movement phase.

Toward Comparative Gendered Social Movement Analysis

The civil rights, Black Power, and anti-apartheid movements can not only be characterized by their dominant sites of struggle, strategies of action, and reactions from the power structure, but comparatively by their particular gender dynamics. From a gendered perspective, the key turning points in racial equality and national liberation movements (NLMs) that define particular stages of struggle can be understood as shifts in the configurations of gender, as well as race, ethnicity, culture, and class. When viewed both within and across movements, each stage can be located by the character of its gender relations, shifts, and struggles. In the cases of the civil rights, Black Power, and anti-apartheid movements, even particular campaigns and actions were intertwined with gender ideologies, inequalities, and power dynamics. The remaining chapters of this book will use a comparative gender analysis to further explore this relationship between gender and social movement mobilization, strategic approaches, and outcomes.

CHAPTER 3

Theorizing Gender in Social Movements

Overview

The discipline of sociology rests on theoretical perspectives that provide guidelines for interpreting and understanding society and social behavior. Social movement theories are frameworks and relational concepts that are specifically geared toward understanding collective actions to change society. They provide the logical frameworks meant to explain social movement emergence, organization, strategies, and likelihood of success. Social movement theories differ in their approaches, areas of emphasis, and levels of analysis. For instance, one ongoing theoretical debate is the relative importance of subjective grievances against the existing order versus objective social conditions in stimulating movement emergence. Another poses the importance of utilitarian or practical versus emotional or sentimental precipitants to action. Moreover, while some perspectives are more concerned with the individual social movement actor, others emphasize the role of movement organizations, resources, and collectivities. These different approaches have implications for the treatment of gender in social movement theory.

Efforts to view these gender dynamics through established social movement theory has led scholars and activists to rethink existing frameworks and develop new gender-conscious approaches. In this chapter, I overview the gendered critiques of established social movement theories and the resultant transformations to which they have been subject. I then apply a synthetic gendered theoretical model to examples from the civil rights, Black Power, and anti-apartheid movements.

Theorizing Social Movements

Until fairly recently, there was a great divide between the ideas of social movement participants and those who studied them. This academic/
activist divide was especially prominent in the 1950s and 1960s, a volatile
period of global social insurgency, resistance, and transformation. During
this time, heightened activity in the civil rights, student, women's, and new
left movements in the United States were paralleled by the rise of national
liberation struggles and socialist revolutions in Africa, Asia, and Latin
America. This volatile time was also characterized by a vast divide between
the militants "in the street" and the scholars in their "ivory towers." For
many movement activists, the academy represented the matrix of hierarchical power relations against which their movements fought.

The movements of this era drew from a variety of belief systems as rationale for and explanation of their struggle. These various ideological
tendencies ranged from the Judeo-Christian religious precepts of morality
and humanity utilized by the civil rights movement to Marxist doctrines
emphasizing class struggle and proletariat revolution that informed the
new left movement. National liberation movements in the "Third World"
and the "nationalist"/Black Power tendency in the U.S. racial equality
movement appropriated revolutionary anti-colonial discourse of thinkers
like Mao Tse Tung and Kwame Nkrumah. All of these ideological perspectives provided the respective movements with an analysis that justified
noninstitutional resistance and insurgency by explaining the cause for their
grievances, providing a guide for strategic action, and proposing a particular desired outcome.

Meanwhile, in the academy, a much different view of social movements
prevailed. The "collective behavior" and "structural strain" approaches,
the earliest attempts to theoretically understand social movements within
the discipline of sociology, saw social movements as aberrational and irrational responses to societal disruption, disorganization, and change (Marx
and McAdam 1994; Smelser 1962). From this social psychological approach,
individuals were thought to engage in social movement activity to vent
feelings of ambiguity and confusion brought on by the strain of these social changes and disruptions such as urbanization, industrialization, and
technological developments. This theoretical perspective was also based
on the assumption of a pluralistic and open political system through which
all interests could be articulated and served. Thus, any noninstitutionalized
strategy for social change was viewed as unnecessary and irrational
(Smelser 1962; McAdam 1982). The causes for social protest were sought

in individual-level anxieties and pathologies, as opposed to structural conditions and power relations.

The dominance of the collective behavior and structural strain models within social movement theory began to crumble in the 1960s and early 1970s. As movement participants and sympathizers entered the academic disciplines, scholarly and activist discourse came closer to each other and, in some cases, even converged.

> Many sociologists felt an affinity with the goals of these movements, and some were active participants in them. When they sought theoretical explanations of these movements, however, they found that existing theories were of limited utility and often contained both inaccurate and unflattering predictions of protest movements and their participants. (Buechler 1993, 218)

In large part, contemporary social movement theory such as resource mobilization, political process models, and new social movement models emerged as a combined critique of the collective behavior approach and validation of the legitimacy of social protest. Opponents of this approach insisted on the political, as opposed to psychological, grounding of social movements (McAdam 1982; Buechler 1993; Wood and Jackson 1982). These social theorists and activists needed more useful and systematic explanations of social movement processes. Their efforts to merge the activist ideologies with social science transformed the sociology of social movements.

Linking Social Movement Theories and Gender: Macro-, Meso-, and Microlevels

In addition to the divide between social movement theory and social activism, scholarly work on gender in social movements underemphasized theory, and social movement theory virtually ignored gender. For the most part, mainstream social movement theories were developed and applied with the assumption of gender neutrality (West and Blumberg 1990). They rarely took gender inequality, structures, or processes—either internal or external to the movement—into account. When social movement theory did address women's experiences or gender, it did so in an oversimplistic manner. This tendency was observed by Verta Taylor and Nancy Whittier:

> Feminist scholars in sociology and other disciplines have been disheartened by the binary oppositions in social movements theory—for example, the

distinction between expressive and instrumental politics, identity and strategic activism, cultural and structural change, and rational and emotional action. (Taylor and Whittier 1999, 5)

On the other hand, the investigations of women in social movements that emerged during the 1970s and 1980s rarely incorporated sociological social movement theories or models. These studies were mostly historical and descriptive. They focused on making women's experience in social struggles visible, rather than on applying theoretical models (Randall 1981; Jaquette 1989, 1994; Freeman 1973). Scholarly works that looked specifically at the experiences of South African women in the anti-apartheid movement such as Diane E. H. Russell's *Lives of Courage: Women for a New South Africa* (1989), Frances Baard and Barbie Schreiner's *My Spirit Is Not Banned* (1986), and Cherryl Walker's *Women and Resistance in South Africa* (1982) fall into this category. Examples of these types of work in the U.S. context are Jo Ann Gibson Robinson's *The Montgomery Bus Boycott and the Women Who Started It* (1987) and Paula Giddings *When and Where I Enter: The Impact of Black Women on Race and Sex in America* (1984).

As sociological research and scholarship became more gender-conscious and gender activists moved into sociology as a discipline, there were increasing attempts to use theory to analyze gendered relations in social movements. These gendered challenges were addressed toward established social movement theories on the macro-, meso-, and microlevels. Macrosociological theories, such as the political process model, which emphasize larger social structural arrangements, are being challenged to take gendered power relations into account. On the mesosociological level, the resource mobilization model, which traditionally focused on the importance of the officially recognized movement structures and resources, is being stretched to appreciate informal groupings and organizational networks that had previously been ignored (McCarthy and Zald 1977; Freeman 1979). New social movement theory stresses the role that collective action frames, collective identities, and cultural symbols play in motivating movement participation (Buechler 1995; Melucci 1985; Snow and Benford 1988; Noonan 1995). These identities and symbols are fused with gendered assumptions and constructs that have to be taken into account.

Some feminist theorists argue against superimposing these preexisting theories onto women and gender in social movements. They argue, instead, that the patterns and systems of understanding should emerge from women's lived experiences (Collins 1990). In this text, I use this type of "emergent theory" to speak back to and undermine the masculinist bias in the established social movement frameworks.

Theorizing gender and social movements has involved a dialectical process of application, critique, synthesis, and transformation. These theoretical shifts not only develop theory that is more relevant to women's experience and take institutionalized gender relations into account, they allow for a greater understanding of social movements overall.

The Political Process Model

The political process model emphasizes the social, political, economic, and subjective conditions that afford a movement the opportunity to emerge and grow. These conditions provide "space" and momentum for social movement mobilization and increase the likelihood of success (McAdam 1982, 1996; Jenkins and Perrow 1977; Tarrow 1983). The political process model makes two important assumptions about social movements: (1) that they are political in nature (vs. a psychological or cultural basis), and (2) that social movements develop in dynamic processes (McAdam 1992). Since this theory approaches social movements as processes, as opposed to static "states," it focuses attention on the shifts and changes in social structures that are necessary, although perhaps not sufficient, for rise in social protest activity. Favorable political opportunities cluster around three factors: shifts in the political opportunity structure, the organizational strength and resources of the insurgents, and the participants' consciousness and perceived probability of success (efficacy).

The political opportunity structure generally refers to the interplay between external societal conditions and/or institutionalized power relations and the social movement within a given nation-state or territory. Commonly cited external dimensions of political opportunity are the relative openness to participation provided within the political system, degree of stability among elite networks, and the capacity for repression on the part of the state structure (McAdam 1982; Tarrow 1996; Staggenberg 1997). Movement conditions are viewed as particularly advantageous during periods of changes in these structures and shifts in the power relations (McAdam 1982; Costain 1992). The ability on the part of the movement to galvanize organizational resources is an additionally necessary condition for the emergence of social protest. Lastly, subjective consciousness and perceived likelihood of success on the part of movement participants interacts with the first two factors to catalyze social insurgency (McAdam 1982).

Three main gendered critiques of the political opportunities approach include (1) its underemphasis on gender as a power relation that contributes to wider political opportunities; (2) its overemphasis on the formal and traditional political realm; and (3) its neglect of the subjective/interpretive aspects of political opportunities (Noonan 1995). With respect to the first critique, an analysis of the larger configuration of social structural and power relations should include the relative positioning of women and men. In what ways do shifts in these patterns precipitate social movement emergence? According to many scholars and activists, shifts in society's power structure differentially impact women's and men's ability to organize which results in "gender differentiated political opportunities." In her analysis of the Palestinian national liberation struggle, Rabab Abdulhadi (1998) attributed the heightened involvement of women to shifts in the women's social status and the growth of the international women's movement globally. The larger society's sociopolitical opportunity structure often has differential mobilizational effects for men and women in movements, as well as the components of movements in which they are involved.

The second critique encourages a view beyond the usual notions of politics, which emphasizes formal sources of power and authority. Applications of the political opportunity model tend to stress the "official" male-dominated spheres of politics (e.g., the state, elite networks, etc.) to the exclusion of other, more female-dominated, areas of social life (e.g., the community, family/kinship networks, etc.). These latter sites are often less structured and visible but are equally necessary organizational and human resources for movement activities. Communication networks and loosely organized collectives were instrumental in the spread of the women's liberation movement of the late 1960s and 1970s in the United States. Steven Buechler (1993) has pointed out in his research that small, nonhierarchically constituted, consciousness-raising groups served as the underlying structural basis for the movement.

The subjective component of the political process model is usually referred to as "cognitive liberation" or perceived effectiveness of resistance. However, critics charge that perceptions about the likelihood of a movement's success are also tied to notions of women's and men's societal roles and positioning. Gender theorists argue that consciousness has to include the ways in which institutionalized gender ideologies interact with larger social conditions to mediate the perception and definition of political opportunities. Constructions of gender can mediate between social conditions and the movement by qualifying "what is" and "what is not" perceived as a political opportunity (Noonan 1995; Lobao 1990; Schild 1994). For example, during the late 1970s and early 1980s, an extremely repressive political period in Latin America, movements of mothers looking for their "disappeared" children and other family members were able to organize and confront the authorities because gender constructs and notions of motherhood made them appear nonthreatening. The idea of political opportunities has to be expanded to include such cultural and ideational factors as gender ideologies.

A gender lens perspective leads to questions such as whether the same political opportunities catalyze activism equally for women and men. To what degree do gendered power relations and roles create or constrain opportunities for activism? How do gender ideologies and meaning systems impact movement strategies and/or likelihood of success? A gendered political process model deepens our understanding of social movements.

Resource Mobilization Theory

Resource mobilization (RM) theory is a social movement framework that emphasizes the organizational structures and tangible resources necessary for social movements to emerge and succeed (McCarthy and Zald 1973, 1977; Jenkins and Perrow 1977; Tilly 1978). This model was also developed as a response to the limitation of the collective behavior and structural strain models (Gurr 1970; Smelser 1962). RM theory counters the assumption that social protest is fundamentally a psychologically driven response to societal disruptions and disorganization. It poses social insurgency as an extension of society's "legitimate" decision-making processes, engaged in by social groups that lack access to the normal channels for political expression (Buechler 1993; Marx and McAdam 1994; McCarthy and Zald 1977; Jenkins and Perrow 1977). Emerging and gaining popularity in the 1970s, this approach emphasized the structured and patterned dynamics of social movements and the rationality of actors within the movement (Oberschall 1973; McCarthy and Zald 1973, 1977; Tilly 1978).

Resource mobilization (RM) theory marked a significant turning point in the scholarship on protest and resistance. It provided a sociological framework for taking social movements seriously as political processes and sites for scholarly research and empirical investigation. In particular, the RM approach argued the importance of organizational and tangible resources (McCarthy and Zald 1973, 1977; Jenkins and Perrow 1977). As initially formulated and routinely applied, the resource mobilization perspective did not explicitly incorporate gender as an analytic category. As a result, two main gendered criticisms of resource mobilization theory have been made: (1) the theory's focus on "official" institutions, structures, and "tangible" resources (Buechler 1993), and (2) the emphasis on the "rational actor" as dichotomously posed against emotion and other subjectivities such as gender ideologies (Ferree 1992).

In contrast to the RM bias in favor of formal organizations and structures, scholars of women in movements have been struck by the impact of informal networks of communication and action on social movement growth and success. For a variety of reasons associated with the gender organization of society and gender division of labor, women often play a more central role in this level of politics (Buechler 1993; Neuhouser 1995; Kaplan 1990). For resource mobilization theory to be gender sensitive, its application must engage and include the "below the surface" and informal networks of power and influence.

The importance of informal networks to the success of the racial/nationalist liberation movements of both South Africa and the United States has been widely documented (Walker 1986; Robnett 1996, 1997; Nauright 1996; Robinson 1987). The gendered division of labor in both movements resulted in male occupation of the official leadership positions (Barnett 1993, 1995; Payne 1990; Robnett 1996, 1997). Women, a large if not majority sector of the movement, established their influence and control mostly through the informal and community-based networks.

As was the case in 1950s South Africa and the southern region of the United States for people of African descent, informal networks are often the only type of social movement form that is able to prosper in highly repressive sociopolitical contexts (Pfaff 1996; Snow, Zurcher, and Ekland-Olson 1980). Pfaff notes that under such authoritarian conditions, "dissent is likely to take the form of small, personalistic groups based on informal ties and loyalties" (Denouex cited in Pfaff 1996, 100). The gendered division of labor in both the public and private realms makes community and kinship networks more accessible to women (Neuhouser 1995; Cable 1992; Gerson and Peiss 1985). In her cross-movement analysis, Kaplan (1990) termed these networks "communities of resistance."

Buechler's (1993) study of European American women in the feminist movement directly conflicted the primacy of formal organizational structures in social movements. He observed that

[t]his organizational bias is particularly evident in the case of the women's movements. To understand these movements, we need the concept of a social movement community (SMC) to designate informally organized networks of movement activists. We need this concept because in the history of women's movements, SMCs have probably played a larger role than SMOs in mobilizing women and pursuing movement goals. (Buechler 1993, 223)

The notions of social movement communities (Buechler 1993), communities of resistance (Kaplan 1990), network centers (Sachs 1988), and political cultures (Kaplan 1990) are different terms for the significance of these previously neglected layers of social struggle in the development and sustenance of movements in general.

The RM model has also been critiqued for not taking the social positioning or structural location of the movement participants into account. According to Myra Marx Ferree, this approaches "pseudo-universalism" in that the social movement participants are seen as

person[s] for whom race, class, gender, and historical circumstances do not determine perceptions in any systematic or socially significant way. In practice, this means that the values and perspectives attributed to everyone are those of white middle-class men in Western capitalist societies. (Ferree 1992, 41)

Scholars have repeatedly pointed out the male bias embedded in this emphasis on the individualist, utilitarian motives for social action to the neglect of the less instrumental and more affective and expressive (Taylor 1995; Foweraker 1995; Buechler 1993; Cohen 1985). According to the "rational actor" perception of movement involvement, "individuals are viewed as weighing the relative costs and benefits of movement participation and opting for participation when the potential benefits outweigh the anticipated costs" (Buechler 1993, 218). The exclusion and devaluation of nonrational/emotional basis for action limits the analysis of social movement activity in a gender-skewed manner. The Mothers of the Plaza de Mayo who organized in Argentina in the aftermath of the 1976 coup, for example, were motivated by the love and emotion generated by their family ties. An application of the resource mobilization theory is inadequate to the extent that it excludes the "more nuanced, relational, communal, nurturant and empathic worlds which is more typical of the female experience" (Buechler 1993, 227).

New Social Movement Theories

New social movement theories, such as collective framing and identity models, reestablished the importance of social psychological and subjective factors in social movement processes. This broad range of theories emphasizes the role of identity formation and symbolic action as central elements of social movement activity and de-emphasizes social structural factors as the basis for resistance activity (Melucci 1985; Foweraker 1995; Buechler 1995). These theorists contend that "new grievances" based on identities and social location that are not necessarily class-based form a contemporary basis for activism (Melucci 1985; Buechler 1995). These perspectives also promote the importance of a sense of collective identity and ideological frames as crucial in linking individuals to resistance struggles (Snow et al. 1986; Snow and Benford 1988).

Taylor and Whittier (1992) and Bernstein (1996), for example, emphasize the development and strategic use of collective and oppositional identity and identities (Bernstein 1996; Noonan 1995) in the social movement process. This process includes the establishment of boundaries that identify and distinguish the collectivity; consciousness and interpretive oppositional ideologies; and negotiation, the interactive process of restructuring symbol or social systems (Taylor and Whittier 1992; Gerson and Peiss 1985).

The fact that new social movement theories emphasize collective identity and social location, both of which are central to the construction of gender, makes them conducive to a gendered analysis, on one level. Other new social movement theorists stress collective action frames as important in the micromobilization process. These frames are the "interpretive schema" or logic that links individuals and their personal experiences to the goals and objectives of a larger social movement (Snow and Benford 1988, 1992; Zald 1996). These action frames are adopted through a process of frame alignment including: (1) frame bridging, the linking of two or more ideologically congruent but unconnected frames regarding an issue; (2) frame amplification, clarification and invigoration of an interpretive frame; (3) frame extension, portraying movement objectives as congruent with values/interests of potential adherents; and (4) frame transformation, a reframing or systematic alteration of accepted or old values or meanings (Snow et al. 1986).

A gendered analysis looks at the ways in which gender ideologies become linked to collective action frames and identities. The "motherist frame" is a good example of how gender ideologies and normative systems are embedded in collective action and identities. Through the "motherist frame" many movements have bridged movement frames that stress the need to fight for equality and justice with the characteristics associated with being a good mother. This frame bridges movement objectives with gender ideology that prescribes that women should be primarily responsible for the safety and welfare of children. Gendered symbols are used to construct this identity that is associated with the movement. However, an intersectional analysis argues that movement participants often occupy several statuses simultaneously, with the importance of any single identity determined, to some degree, by the context (Brewer 1993; King 1988).

This frame-bridging process can also work the other way around. In the application of the collective action frame model to social movements described above, the focus is on movement organizations connecting their "framing" of the situation to belief systems that potential participants already hold. Approaches to movements that have stressed subjective motivations for social movement involvement have been convinced of the importance of perceptions and other ideational factors in stimulating social resistance efforts (Melucci 1985; Snow and Benford 1988, 1992). Ideas, cultural elements, symbolism, and shared meanings/ideologies have been key variables in these investigations. Not only do socially embedded constructions of gender impact the justifications for protest, gender is also constructed and reconstructed in the process of movement participation.

Emergent Theory from Movement Lives

Scholars' and activists' gendered analyses of social movements have been in the forefront of synthesizing theoretical perspectives. Noonan (1995), for example, combines the political process and collective action frame models to capture the workings of gender in the Chilean movement. Ferree and Miller (1985) have suggested a combined approach that takes resources and rationality as well as ideology and subjectivity into account in order to reduce the masculinist bias in social movement analysis that has devalued the impact of subjectivity and emotion and ignored informal and submerged networks and resistance communities. Gendered theoretical approaches have combined the various components of traditional social movement theories that best address gender and social movements.

Some gender-conscious social movement theorists and activists argue that theory should emerge organically from the experience of women and men in particular movements. Patricia Hill Collins (1990) refers to knowledge production that is developed from the lived experiences of women "standpoint epistemology." From this perspective, women's experiences, in particular, are viewed as a location for theorizing about the relationship of gender to social resistance movements (Collins 1990; Sharoni 1995). Simona Sharoni states:

> Since women are not a monolithic group, any single framework will not be sufficient to capture the complexity and the different dimensions and particularities of their struggles. In other words, we need to move beyond typologies and into the complex realms and locations where women actually make history and theory . . . to theorize about women's resistance in this context cannot emerge in academic settings and then be applied to case studies. (Sharoni 1995, 29)

In this way, theorizing gender in social movements becomes a back-and-forth between theory and women's actual lived experiences. This dialectical process results in "emergent theory," frameworks and models that actively emerge from the standpoints of women within particular social contexts and in concert with race, ethnicity, culture, and class.

Such approaches build on the gendered critiques, draw from the theoretical strengths, and offset the limitations of social movement theories. In the analysis that follows, I combine ideas from gendered political process/opportunities resource mobilization (RM) and new social movement (NSM) theories where appropriate and relevant. I also draw from women's lived experiences, or emergent theory, to transform and transcend these models.

Gendered Political Opportunities, Resources, and Identities: The Anti-Pass Campaign and the Montgomery Bus Boycott

The gendered critiques of the political process, resource mobilization, and new social movement model can be illustrated and applied through analyses of the racial/national liberation movement in the South African and U.S. contexts. The existence and interpretation of political opportunities for social resistance, in both cases, was related to the differential experiences and structural locations of women and men within the context of race/class-based systems of power and inequality (Barnett 1993, 1995; Robnett 1996, 1997; Walker 1982). The gender ideologies inherent in the cultures both constrained and catalyzed particular social movement activities in ways that implicated gender, race, and class. These gender-differentiated political opportunities, resources, and identities were evident in both the South African and U.S. social movement cases.

Political Opportunity Structures

Distinct political opportunities for resistance can open up as a result of shifts in society's gender structure and associated power relations. This was the case with respect to South African women in the 1950s. The anti-pass campaign, which was initiated by the Federation of South African Women (FSAW), had its basis in the gendered nature of the apartheid state structure and migratory labor system. At a time when the ability for African people to engage in "legitimate" political processes, already severely limited, closed even further, women found the opportunity and space to mobilize. In response to the African National Congress (ANC)-sponsored Defiance Campaign of civil disobedience in 1952, in which apartheid laws were consciously disobeyed, the South African government responded by jailing more than 800,000 people, using violence to suppress the resistance and banning meetings of movement organizations (Baard 1986). These conditions, characterized as strengthened governmental power and a repressive state, would normally be associated with unfavorable political opportunities for the growth of a movement. However, even at this low point for male-led national liberation activities, women and women's organizations were able to increase their anti-apartheid activities (Kimble and Unterhalter 1982; Seidman 1993; Walker 1982; Wells 1993). These same shifts in the political opportunity structure that constrained male-led organizations like the African National Congress and the South African Communist Party were favorable for the resistance activities engaged in by women.

Gendered shifts in the patterns of urbanization and labor organization during that period of South African history were particularly conducive to women's resistance activities (Wells 1993). While still disproportionately relegated to the poverty-stricken Bantustans and native homelands outside of the towns, African women were increasingly present in urban areas and the shantytowns directly adjacent to them during the 1940s and 1950s (Berger 1990; Wells 1993). Working primarily as domestic servants, petty traders, and seasonal workers in the food industry, African women workers had greater autonomy in some areas than their male counterparts.

For a time, African women were also able to participate in union organizing that was denied to African men based on the construction of female and male roles in the private and public spheres. Based on the patriarchal assumptions embedded in racist South African law, a loophole in apartheid legislation forbade African men, but not women, from union organizing. Since the migratory labor system had been designed to attract cheap male labor to the gold and diamond mines and assumed that women would remain in the homelands, only men were required to carry passes. The passbook, as an instrument of land and labor control, was also a marker and mechanism for the social construction and control of both race and gender (Barnes 1997). The Industrial Conciliation Act of 1924 forbade union organizing among "pass-bearing natives," a category to which African women did not belong until 1954.

> An historic court case—Christina Okolo vs. the Industrial Council for the Clothing Industry, Transvaal—succeeded in establishing African women's right to belong to registered unions by proving that they did not fall within the definition of "pass-bearing" worker as laid down in the Industrial Conciliation Act. In other words, they were eligible for all the benefits of union membership and industrial legislation that non-African workers enjoyed. (Walker 1982, 120)

The changing gender dynamics in the workforce and urban area residence, coupled with gender-biased legislation, allowed women activists like Frances Baard, later a leader in the anti-pass campaign, to gain political experience as a leader in the Food and Canning Workers Union and the Garment Workers Union (Baard 1986; Berger 1990; Mashinini 1991; Walker 1982).

At the same time that the urban migration of women resulted in a larger than desired urban African population, it created labor shortages in rural areas. To maintain control in the midst of these transformations, the Nationalist party announced that the pass laws would be extended to women. Cherryl Walker explains the reason that extension of pass laws affected women so significantly:

> In the state of flux and uncertainty that surrounded the urban family, the position of women was often contradictory, their status confused. On the one hand, women tended to gain in independence and authority. In many cases they were playing the strongest part in holding their families together, an important factor in explaining why the opposition of African women to pass laws was always so deeply felt. (Walker 1982, 149)

In response, activist African women and women-led organizations sprang into action in 1953, the year following the announcement of pass extensions to women (Walker 1982; Beall, Hassim, and Todes 1989; Nauright 1996). A small group of women met in Port Elizabeth to discuss the implications of the extension of pass laws to women. They organized autonomously by forming the Federation of South African Women (FSAW), in part because of limitations on the roles that women could play in the official anti-apartheid organizations. The strategic focus and mass actions of women altered the political environment and opportunity structure significantly. Following the women's example, the established national liberation organizations, the African National Congress (ANC) and the Congress Alliance (a coalition of other national liberation organizations), then took up the anti-pass cause as a movement focus.

In the case of the U.S. civil rights movement, it is not a coincidence that the precipitating event in the Montgomery Bus Boycott was the arrest of Mrs. Rosa Parks, a middle-class African American woman, nor that the initial organizers of the boycott were women. During that period in U.S. history, a large proportion of African American women in Montgomery, Alabama, worked as domestic servants. As Judy Aulette and Walda Katz Fishman observed,

> The bus boycott was not only begun by a woman, it was also led by women, supported by women, and addressed a problem that was most salient for black women. The deplorable treatment of patrons of public transportation in Montgomery was of critical importance to black working class women because they were likely to be employed as domestics across town from their homes. They were the main customers, therefore, of the public transportation system. (Aulette and Katz Fishman 1991, 4)

In addition to the gendered nature of the labor force and transportation clientele, women and men had different experiences on the bus lines. The most violent repression for challenging the segregationist practices were reserved for African American men. In 1952, an African American man named Brooks was killed by police while getting off the bus after an exchange of hostile words with the bus driver. These direct assaults proved particularly damaging, given accepted notions of "manhood" associated with the male role as protector. As Jo Ann Gibson Robinson, president of the Women's Political Council (WPC) during that time, remembers:

> The number of Negro men walking increased during 1954 and early 1955. They walked to and from work, to town, to movies, to see their girlfriends, because of fear of riding the buses. (Robinson 1987, 37)

Gender dynamics within the established movement organizations also limited the ability for women to respond to their concerns. The Women's Political Council (WPC) was formed in 1946, in part because of the gender bias in the mainstream organizations for racial equality (e.g., the NAACP, SCLC, etc.). According to founder Mary Fair Burks, the WPC excluded men because of the possibility that they "would take it over and women wouldn't be able to do what they could do" (quoted in Robnett 1997, 56). Thus, while the WPC did not pursue gender-related objectives, its autonomy from the mainstream race equity organizations of the movement proved to be a crucial factor in the construction of a favorable political opportunity structure. While women were members of many civil rights organizations, their role was viewed as supportive.

The WPC had been planning a bus boycott as a potential strategy for months before the actual boycott. Positioned to initiate a response, they had become impatient with the gradualist approach of the established leadership:

> The women intuited danger in their men's tiredness, in the limits of the children's and their own endurance. . . . They were ready to boycott. On paper, the WPC had already planned for fifty thousand notices calling people to boycott the buses; only the specifics of time and place had to be added. And, as tempers flared and emotions ran high, the women became active. (Robinson 1987, 39)

A gendered appreciation for political opportunities, then, forces an expansion of the dimensions contributing to favorable movement conditions in the United States as well as South Africa. In both the anti-pass and bus boycott cases, the gender patterns of urban workforce and constraints within movement organizations provided a political opportunity for women-led activism. This activism, in turn, transformed the political opportunity structure. The gendered dynamics of the wider social structure from which movements emerge and the internal movement gender dynamics both play a part in shaping political opportunities.

Women as Indigenous Organizational Resources

A gendered critique of both the political process and resource mobilization models is the bias toward formal organizations and structures. The importance of informal networks of communication and action, particularly with respect to women's activism, is often lost to these approaches. Because of the caretaking work that women perform and their limited access to official leadership positions within social movement organizations, women often focus their activism on more grassroots and mass levels (Barnett 1993; Neuhouser 1995; Robnett 1996, 1997). For the political process model to be gender sensitive, the assessment of "indigenous organizational strength" must include informal networks.

Autonomous women's organizations in the civil rights movement paralleled and supported the better known civil rights organizations. In the scholarly treatments of the civil rights movement, groups such as the Club from Nowhere and the Friendly Club are rarely mentioned or are discussed only in brief (McAdam 1992; Morris 1984). The fact that women held multiple and overlapping memberships in organizations and networks was instrumental in facilitating communication, galvanizing financial and human resources, and coordinating action. The importance of informal networks and kinship relations to women's involvement in both struggles is part of the gender dialectic of the South African and U.S. racial/national liberation movements. These collectivities paralleled, countered, and often challenged the more male-dominated official social movement organizations and structures.

Cognitive Liberation and Gendered Consciousness

"Cognitive liberation," the collective assessment of the prospects for successful insurgency, is a crucial aspect of movement consciousness. This sense of efficacy cannot exist in a vacuum, but must be linked to other meaning systems, ideologies, and identities, including those associated with gender. The subjective meanings that people attach to their situations mediate between political opportunity and action strategies (McAdam 1982). Gender ideologies are often incorporated in movement collective action frames, the interpretive linkage between the individual and the social movement (Snow and Benford 1988, 1992; Zald 1996). New social movement (NSM) theory and collective action-framing models have emphasized the role of identity formation and the strategic use of collective and oppositional identities in resistance movements (Bernstein 1996).

The "motherist frame," a justification for social action based on the mothering attributes of nurturance and responsibility for the family that are part of the construction of womanhood, was used in both the anti-pass campaign and Montgomery Bus Boycott (Noonan 1995; Schirmer 1993). This frame has also been referred to as politicized motherhood, activist mothering, and politicized domesticity. In the anti-pass campaign, the rationale for women's resistance to the passes was fundamentally based around their roles as women, wives, and mothers (FSAW 1958; Walker 1982; Lodge 1983). FSAW appealed to women to join the marches to Pretoria on the basis of their duty as women and mothers. A pamphlet titled a "Call To Mothers" was a rallying cry and stated:

> Our children's future depends on the extent to which we, the mothers of South Africa, organise and work and fight for a better life for our little ones. (FSAW, n.d.[a])

The women used their roles and duties associated with being wives and mothers as justification for their resistance against passes. The literature used in the anti-pass campaign to galvanize action even pictures a mother and child, posing movement activity as a valid "mothering" response to the danger imposed by apartheid on children. Posing motherhood as a basis for political action and political action as a motherly obligation has been utilized to draw women into a variety of social movements.

The civil rights movement does not offer as clear-cut a usage of the mother identity as a conscious mobilizing frame. However, the identity and role of the "mother" was important. In her discussion of the civil rights movement, Sara Evans (1979) asserted the importance of the "mama" who took care of activists from other places, was militant, outspoken, and community focused.

Gendered Social Movement Theory: From Application and Critique to Transformation

As the South African and U.S. examples illustrate, gender can be a central point from which to critique and identify gaps in social movement theory. It facilitates the development of theory organically from the experience of women and men in particular movements. Through a gender lens, women's struggles are a location for theorizing. The political process model can be a useful theoretical framework from which to understand gender and social movements, if the concept of political opportunities is expanded to include shifts in gendered power dynamics. Resource mobilization theorists have to look beyond formal organizations and tangible resources. New social movement theorists must assess the gendered identities and symbols utilized in social movement processes.

Using gender as a conceptual hinge for theorizing social movements has exposed Eurocentric, middle-class male biases lurking in frameworks and perspectives assumed to be universal, or at least universally applied (Kaplan 1990; Ferree 1992; Noonan 1995; Robnett 1996, 1997). The application and critique of social movement theory through a gender lens has expanded and transformed our knowledge about social movements and gender both generally, and as expressed in particular national, class, and cultural contexts and historical junctures.

CHAPTER 4

"Getting Fired Up":
Gendered Factors in Movement Mobilization

Albany was not simply a student movement. There were just swarms of people who came out to demonstrate, from high school students to old people. And there was so much that you got from finding that some older people backed you . . . . That made the Movement much stronger. It was a mass movement. (Bernice Johnson Reagon quoted in Levy 1992, 98)

The Question of Mobilization

Bernice Johnson Reagon's memory of the sit-ins in Albany, Georgia, in 1964 describes the "heyday" of a movement. In this peak period of the U.S. civil rights movement, masses of individuals were swept into or affected by the social change activities. During the most active periods of the anti-apartheid, civil rights, and Black Power movements, individuals who had not previously been involved became movement participants, new organizations and movement structures emerged, and ideologies and collective action frames were refined and disseminated. Reagon's description highlights the widespread nature of a movement during a period of heightened mobilization. Even though engaged in by only a small fraction of the potential beneficiaries of the movement, its organizations and confrontational actions "spread like wildfire." For instance, within just a month after the first well-known sit-in in Greensboro, North Carolina, sit-ins had spread to thirty-one other cities in the South (Morris 1984). In South Africa's anti-pass campaign, one thousand protesters grew to ten thousand over the span of ten months.

Social movement scholars and activists have been extremely interested in identifying the social conditions that stimulate the emergence of large-scale rebellion against established power structures. From the perspective of movement organizations and leaders, social transformation often hinges on the question of mobilization. What social conditions or changes in social conditions stimulate action? How do organizations get individuals motivated or "fired up" enough to participate in the movement-building activities that, by definition, go against the grain and challenge the status quo? Why do people make long-term commitments, risk their livelihoods, and place themselves in potentially dangerous situations for the greater good of the collective?

There are no simple or straightforward relationships between the existence of social injustice and oppression and the rise of resistance and movement mobilization. One does not necessarily follow the other. Oppressive, exploitative, and unjust conditions can persist for long periods of time with low levels of organized or sustained efforts to change them. In fact, the relative deprivation model popularized by Ted Gurr in the 1970s argues that social protest is more likely to develop as a result of improving conditions which increase expectations (Gurr 1970). This and other theories of micromobilization have sought to explain the relationship between social conditions and movement mobilization.

To a large degree, questions and proposed answers to questions surrounding mobilization have been framed in ways that refer to a generalized population of movement participants. However, according to Lilia Rodriguez,

> Gender differences are crucial in understanding why and how women and men organize and participate in urban struggle. Women and men perform different roles, have distinct needs, social responsibilities, expectations, and power, and are socialized in different ways. Gender as a social construction explains the social relations between men and women, which are dialectic and vary with class, race, culture, age, religion, and so on, and it explains their differential participation. (Rodriguez 1994, 34)

As Rodriguez implies, movement mobilization is steeped with gendered effects, although the relationship between institutionalized gender and movement mobilization varies given the particular conditions. Grievances about social conditions do not automatically turn into full-scale social movements but are dependent on the existence of a particular combination of factors to congeal and come together. What are these factors? The discussion that follows begins to identify some of them.

Through a gender lens, questions surrounding movement mobilization have a different slant. The interest may be in how social conditions differentially motivate men and women to become involved in social resistance movements. To what extent and in what ways are the organizations and networks that pull people into the movement (i.e., mobilizing structures) differentiated by gender? How do organizations use assumptions about gender, either consciously or unconsciously, to stimulate participation? Once recruited, do women and men play different roles in the mobilization process? This chapter draws upon the political process model by addressing these questions using a multidimensional and gendered framework that treats mobilization as the dynamic interplay of conducive factors on the social structural (macro), organizational (meso), and individual (micro) levels.

Earlier scholarship on the relationship between gender and mobilization focused on the "structural constraints" that differentially imposed barriers to women's participation as a result of the skewed sexual division of labor. Scholars and activists were, often with good cause, concerned with the limitations on movement involvement placed on women as a result of the constraints of disproportionate child rearing and domestic responsibilities (Cable 1992; Machel 1980; Sankara 1988). While these barriers certainly existed, more recent scholarship delves deeper and seeks to understand the more complex interactions in which gender asymmetries, divisions of labor, and power differentials serve as both impediments and catalysts to movement involvement (Neuhouser 1995).

Gender and Social Movement Mobilization: The Macrolevel Dimension

Macrosociological factors in social movement mobilization are those broader material conditions and shifts in the sociopolitical or economic environment that stimulate or constrain movement involvement (McAdam 1982; McAdam et al. 1996; Jenkins and Perrow 1977; Tarrow 1995). As described in the earlier discussion of political opportunity structures, this broader level can include the distribution or maldistribution of social resources, political power inequities, and divisions of labor. The emergence of a social movement is prompted by the existence of favorable opportunities on the political, economic, social, and cultural levels. Also necessary is the reduction of impediments for collective resistance that exist in the external society, such as isolation of potential activists from each other and /

or the threat of governmental repression and attack (Marx 1982). In addition to the real or perceived social inequalities or injustices that exist, there must be ample opportunity to collectivize resistance activities.

In most societies, women and men experience these broader structural conditions differently. Historically developed gender divisions that situate women and men at particular locations within the socioeconomic and political system, community, and family are manifested in social movement mobilization. For instance, although both women and men were subject to economic exploitation, political disempowerment, and limited opportunities as a result of the systems of Jim Crow in the United States and apartheid in South Africa, the particular way in which they were affected differed. As we have seen, although African male workers in South Africa had been required to carry passes since 1913, the anti-pass campaign did not emerge until the 1950s when women were forced to carry them. Similarly, the expressions of resistance against racial segregation on the Montgomery, Alabama, bus lines prior to the 1955 bus boycott initiated by the Women's Political Council (WPC) had been sporadic and unorganized.

Each of these mobilization opportunities generated distinct incentives, levels, and sites of movement engagement for women and men. In both cases, the racial, ethnic, and class stratification system interacted with patriarchal relations in ways that radicalized and mobilized women at different levels and incorporated them into the movement in distinctive ways (Magubane 1979; McAdam 1982; Wells 1993). Movement mobilization is affected by gendered opportunities to politically mobilize and differentiated precipitating issues around which women and men mobilized.

Saving Crossroads

In the case of South Africa, the relative structural locations of women vis-à-vis men in the labor market may have constrained union activism and production-based struggles, but it provided opportunities for mobilizing on community levels and in residence-based struggles. The struggle to "Save Crossroads" provides an example of how these gendered factors came together in both catalytic and constraining ways with respect to social movement mobilization on the community level. The convergence of these forces at the Crossroads camp beginning in the 1970s centralized the role of gendered relationships in stimulating movement participation.

Crossroads was a squatter community at the South African Cape Peninsula that began developing in the mid-1960s. As a result of apartheid legislation and the sex-segregated housing practices of most of the industries for which the male migrants worked, the majority of the residents of Crossroads were African women and children who had made their way to urban areas and were forced to establish "illegal" residence in the shantytowns and townships adjacent to urban and industrial areas. From the perspective of the South African government, the Crossroads women held a marginal status on several counts. They were defined by apartheid legislation as "legal" residents of their rural homelands, as opposed to the urban areas in which they resided. As such, they had no legal or political rights as citizens. According to Josette Cole, only 9.3 percent of the women in Crossroads had "legal rights" to be there according to apartheid laws. As workers in private households or in the informal and underground economy, or as unemployed spouses or mates of male laborers, they did not even have the minimal status as "workers."

The gendered migration, urbanization, and industrialization patterns in South Africa in the early part of the nineteenth century played a significant role in catalyzing anti-apartheid mobilization. Initially, rural to urban migration in South Africa consisted mostly of men leaving the rural areas and homelands to find work in the mines and budding industries. They were discouraged from bringing their families by apartheid legislation that restricted urban residence to officially documented workers, a category which specifically excluded women and children. According to the Urban Areas Acts of 1923 and 1945, "'natives' were only permitted into municipal areas for labour purposes" (Cole 1987, 5). In addition, African men who were employed in the mines or other industry were often required to reside in single-sex hostels and worker compounds.

Despite these restrictions, African women moved from the overcrowded and barren rural homelands to urban areas like Johannesburg and Capetown in greater and greater numbers leading up to the organized resistance. In less than forty-five years, the sex ratio among the urban African population narrowed from 20 males to every 1 female in 1911 to 1.8-to-1 by 1946 (Wells 1993). The exodus of women from the rural areas and homelands was the result of "push factors" such as poverty, lack of employment, and lack of economic opportunities. On the other side, the lure of employment and reuniting with family members and mates who had already migrated to the cities, and escape from repressive cultural restrictions on them as women, were "pull" factors. Most African women who moved to urban areas were forced to establish residence in the shantytowns, temporary settlements, and townships adjacent to urban and industrial areas. These compounded marginalities made the Crossroads women particularly vulnerable to police harassment and governmental attacks.

The apartheid regime viewed the migration of women to the urban areas as particularly dangerous on several counts. For one thing, the reunification of families increased the likelihood of permanent African urban settlement being formed. In addition, the urban migration of African women from the rural areas left Afrikaner/Boer farmers with a shortage of African female labor who had, up until that point, comprised a large portion of the agricultural and seasonal labor since working-age men had been more attracted to the mines and urban industry. According to Julia Wells, "the unregulated flow of rural Black women into the towns became especially threatening to [white] farmers" (Wells 1993, 115). In addition, municipal authorities in the urban areas were alarmed by their inability to curtail the massive entry into the townships. Finally, the White business interests found it difficult to control African women's labor because of their predominance in informal and underground areas of work that were outside the official labor force, such as beer brewers, handicraft and food producers, or street vendors. This was one of the main conditions that facilitated women's mobilization.

In addition to the extension of pass requirements to women during the 1950s and 1960s, aggressive relocation efforts were pursued by the apartheid government to gain control over African women's labor and residence (Wells 1993). These initiatives expressed a unity between, and served the economic and political interests of, the White business and agricultural elites in South Africa (Wells 1993). From the 1950s through the 1980s, the South African government intensified their pass raids and the forced removal of thousands of residents from the urban townships and squatters' camp.

In February of 1975, the residents of Crossroads received official notice that they were going to be evicted and/or relocated (Cole 1987; Kaplan 1997). This precipitating incident was followed by pass raids in which hundreds of residents were harassed and jailed for pass law violations. The community responded by forming parallel but separate Women's and Men's Crossroads Committees to counter governmental removals. The Women's Committee took the leading role in the struggle against the evictions as a result of their central positioning and large numbers of women within the community. According to Cole, "these women, either unemployed or employed in the informal sector and therefore more in touch with day to day problems, slowly developed into a much more powerful force within Crossroads than either of the Men's Committees" (Cole 1987, 20). Within a month, the Women's Crossroads Committee sent a delegation of thirty women to the Athlone Advice Office, a legal assistance project of Black Sash, the liberal White women's anti-apartheid organization, to solicit help in countering governmental encroachments. One of the workers in the office remembered this as a critical moment in the struggle.

> "Until 1975 when you did everything you could to get permission for a woman to stay, and you failed, she went. But the women of Crossroads were the first women to sit in our office and say—'we are not going.'" (quoted in Cole 1987, 14)

Between 1975 and 1978, the Crossroads Women's Committee consolidated their efforts at the same time the Men's Committee split and became internally divisive. The Women's Committee engaged in a diversified set of actions to bring attention to their plight. They hired lawyers in a legal fight against the Cape Town Divisional Council, raised bail money for those arrested during pass raids, started community educational programs, and formed work teams to clean up the area. They spread the word about the impending destruction of their community both nationally and internationally through a multifaceted "Stand Up for Crossroads" campaign, which involved a touring dramatization titled *Imfuduso (The Exodus)*, creating and distributing bumper stickers and cards, publishing editorials in local newspapers, and presenting a photo exhibition. As a result of their efforts, the Women's Committee succeeded in having Crossroads declared an Emergency Camp in 1976, which allowed for the provision of basic services such as water taps and sewage services. This victory was temporary in nature, however, as residents were eventually forced out of what became "old" Crossroads in 1986.

Despite the limited nature of these short-term gains, the "Save Crossroads" campaign had long-lasting impact. The activism of the Women's Committee forestalled governmental efforts to forcibly remove Crossroads residents for more than a decade, provided an organizational basis for the squatters' rights movement, and framed grievances around housing and living conditions in a manner that would inform efforts later in the movement. The "Save Crossroads" campaign was a clear example of a social movement moving from more spontaneous activities and decentralized structure to more formal organization. The campaign activists went on to create a standing Surplus People Project which continues to struggle for squatter's rights. Regina Ntongana, president of the Crossroads Women's Committee in 1976, was a co-founder of this organization.

Boycotting Buses

As discussed earlier, migration and labor force organization also played a part in creating the macrolevel conditions for mobilization in the U.S. civil rights movement. The demographic shifts in spatial location of African Americans in the beginning of the twentieth century also contributed to the mobilization of African Americans in the civil rights movement. According to Doug McAdam (1982), the great migration of African Americans out of the South and from rural to urban areas provided opportunity for mobilization. It played a role in shifting the north-south balance of power, strengthened the African American political presence, and provided opportunities for the development of strong institutions such as the NAACP and Black churches.

The occupational stratification by race and gender in the United States, which created a "racial division of reproductive labor" or domestic service, was significant in precipitating the rise of the modern civil rights movement (Aulette and Fishman 1993; Glenn 1997). African American women in the South during this time were also employed predominantly in the service industry as domestics. According to the U.S. Bureau of the Census, African American women were employed in private service at the rate of 58.1 percent in 1940 and 46.4 percent by 1960 (U.S. Commission on Civil Rights 1990). Unlike their South African counterparts, African American males were latecomers to industrial work; instead, they were heavily skewed toward unskilled manual labor and farm work (Fredrickson 1981; Giddings 1984). At the same time, Jim Crow legislation and practices that racially segregated all areas of social life in the South kept African Americans and European Americans separated from each other spatially.

The need for African American women who worked as domestic servants to commute to the residential White areas increased their dependence on and thus their investment in public transportation. African American female domestics comprised the largest proportion of intra-urban migrants between the Black and White neighborhoods in southern U.S. cities during the 1950s. It is no accident, then, that over two-thirds of the boycotters were women. In this instance, the structural location of African American women in the labor market as domestic servants opened a particular path of action. The strength of their numbers was the basis for the success of the Montgomery Bus Boycott.

Gender as institutionalized in the political, economic, and social structure factored into the rural-to-urban and intra-urban migration, the racialized labor market segmentation, and racial residential segregation, which precipitated movement emergence and impacted the gender composition of the mobilizing resistance in the Crossroads and Montgomery Boycott cases. As the anti-apartheid and civil rights cases illustrate, gendered and racialized divisions of labor in the society impact the particular lines of communication and sites of interaction that draw women and men into social movements, that is, mobilization paths. Gender contributes to the broader conditions leading to social resistance in both the movements in a myriad of ways.

Networks and Mobilizing Structures: The Mesolevel

On the mesolevel, social movement mobilization is facilitated by social networks and organizations through which individuals funnel their efforts toward social change. Mobilizing structures are the sites for transmitting movement ideas, coordinating activities, and, most importantly, drawing participants into the movement. These networks and organizations provide the paths through which potential movement beneficiaries and sympathizers are galvanized to confront the power structures and systems of inequality they seek to transform. In addition, "mobilizing structures" mediate between the movement objectives and participants, use various strategies to recruit and involve movement participants, and find and coordinate resources.

Mobilizing structures can range from being loosely bound collectives that operate relatively informally to those that are more highly structured and formally recognized. For instance, the networks of communication that initially existed in the South African community of Crossroads and among members of the congregations in the African American churches, which played significant roles in building the movements, are examples of less formalized structures. On the other hand, entities like the Montgomery Improvement Association, the Women's Political Council, and the Surplus People Project are examples of formal structures that mobilized movement participation (Cole 1987; McAdam 1982; Morris 1984). Some mobilizing structures employ centralized, top-down, and hierarchical decision-making processes while others lean toward egalitarianism and collective or rotating leadership. Whether formal or informal, pre-established and already existing social networks provide the paths for movement mobilization (Cable 1992; McAdam 1982; Snow, Zurcher, and Elkand-Olson 1980). The established lines along which people interact determine movement participation flow, in great part. In fact, large-scale movement interaction occurs mostly through the consolidation and coordination of existing social networks and structures (Oberschall 1973; McAdam 1982). It follows, then, that movement participants will tend to organize in the locations they find themselves: the workplace, the community, and/or the family. Some of these networks are formal and officially recognized, such as in the labor force or educational system, while others are more informal and loosely structured. The most extreme example of this process is "bloc recruitment" when whole existing organizations or networks are absorbed into the social movement.

The networks and structures that impact movement mobilization are embedded in the gendered nature of the social order. Differences in the lives of women and men, and in their social location and interaction, contour their involvement in specific types of movement networks and structures and the hierarchies and power differences within these entities. There are also numerous ways in which mobilizing structures differentiate by gender and exhibit gender distinctions, hierarchies, and asymmetries. Gender differences in social location create particular lines of communication and sites of interaction that draw women and men into the movement along different paths and, sometimes, into separate organizations or structures. For example, in a study of correspondence sent by movement participants to Dr. Martin Luther King Jr. during the 1960s, Platt and Fraser (1998) found that women's letters reflected connection to the movement via personal relationships, as opposed to men's letters that stressed networking through institutional ties and external connections.

At the initial point of contact, women and men are often treated differently in the recruitment process. Once recruited, the roles of women and men, particularly with respect to mobilizing other participants, are often separate and placed in rank order with respect to attention and value. There are also differences in their relative utilization of formal versus informal mobilizing structures. Until very recently, these factors combined to seriously underestimate the contributions that women have made in mobilizing mass support in social movements.

Gender-Differentiated Recruitment into Formal Movement Structures

The tendency for formal movement structures to differentially mobilize and recruit female versus male participation is the first point of gender differentiation in movement structures. In his gendered analysis of the Student Nonviolent Coordinating Committee's (SNCC) selection process for participants in the Freedom Summer project, sociologist Doug McAdam (1992) observed "differential recruitment" on the basis of gender and race which posed barriers to the recruitment of women relative to men. Freedom Summer was the 1964 civil rights movement offensive in which mostly European American/White college students from the urban North were recruited into SNCC to engage in a massive voter registration drive in the South. McAdam's research revealed that female applicants were more likely than men to have been "rejected for participation or . . . , despite being accepted, failed to take part in the project" (McAdam 1992, 1217). This was the case despite the fact that the female applicants had higher levels of previous civil rights activism and greater numbers of organizational affiliations overall, both of which were major selection criteria for inclusion in the project. However, the gendered results of the recruitment efforts indicate that, in many cases, the criteria used to select women and men differed.

Reports by interviewers revealed numerous sexual "double standards" that were applied in the selection process. For instance, with female applicants, more than with their male counterparts, the issue of sex was broached in interviews and comments on their physical attractiveness alluded to in interview reports. McAdam speculates that since most of these female applicants were White, the basis for this line of questioning rested in the larger context of racism and sexist stereotypes. Specifically, the myth of the African American/Black male as sexual predator and rapist that served as justification for racist violence in the South was drawn upon. The counterpart of this image of the Black sexually aggressive male is that of African American/Black female promiscuity, which are both juxtaposed against the constructions of White female purity and victimization. As Angela Davis has observed, "the fictional image of the Black man as rapist has always strengthened its inseparable companion: the image of the Black woman as chronically promiscuous" (Davis 1983). These racist and sexist assumptions and underlying fears of interracial interaction factored into the Freedom Summer recruitment. Recruiters and the family members of potential participants were especially sensitive to the potential for sexual relationships with African American men and other potential dangers that might befall European American/White women (Davis 1983; McAdam 1992). In McAdam's words, "Certainly, the dangerous, unchaperoned, interracial, and political character of the project posed more a threat to femaleness than maleness" (McAdam 1992, 1219).

These racialized and gendered constructs were also evident in the other major distinction between female and male applicants—the greater parental resistance to women's participation. This resistance was reflective of the particular limitations on the acceptable roles available to women at that time. This narrowness was also reflected in the way in which notions of the appropriate division of labor between women and men informed recruitment. Many female applicants were rejected from the project outright on the basis of their work preferences. Specifically, women who expressed concern about, or were opposed to, merely doing clerical and supportive movement tasks characteristic of the normative female roles in the interview were rejected.

> For the male applicant, participation in a project like Freedom Summer could be functionally equivalent to any number of other traditional challenges that were available to young men as part of the process of "becoming a man." ... There were few, if any equivalent precedents available to the female volunteers to legitimate their participation in the project." (McAdam 1992, 1218)

In the South African case, barriers to movement participation on the part of women based in gender ideologies often came from male relatives and husbands who viewed activism as outside the realm of women's work. In the Report of the First National Conference of Women held in Johannesburg, South Africa, in 1954, Lillian Ngoyi of the African National Congress (ANC) was applauded when she stated that "if it had not been for the husbands, who kept back many of the women, we would have many more delegates at this Conference. The husbands talked of democracy, but did not practice it" (FSAW 1954, 9). As a reaction to these constraints to their movement involvement, African women adopted gender-specific mobilizing strategies. The Federation of South African Women (FSAW) and Congress of Mothers specifically recruited women into the anti-pass campaign and anti-apartheid movement using their roles and duties as mothers as incentive. In this way, women engaged in subversive activity that simultaneously resisted the patriarchy of apartheid state as well as their husbands and fathers using the socially acceptable role of "mother." While the Federation was able to use this underlying logic as a basis from which to mobilize thousands of women in anti-pass demonstrations, campaigns, and direct actions in the 1955–1958 period, this same logic was used by the official movement organization leadership to undermine and contain women's activism at the point that it reached its zenith. When thousands of women packed the jails of Johannesburg in a 1958 series of anti-pass direct actions, the Joint Women's Executives met and decided that "no further bail should be paid and that demonstrations to the pass office should continue as long as the support for the women could be maintained" (FSAW 1958, 2). This position was overruled by the male-led ANC executive who argued that there was insufficient preparation for their actions and voted to bail the protesters out of jail. Researchers Judy Kimble and Elaine Unterhalter (1982) speculate that their position was "influenced by sexual politics. Given the sexual division of labour the absence of wives and mothers from households threw extra responsibilities on fathers and husbands" (Kimble and Unterhalter 1982, 27). It is no coincidence that many of these ANC leaders were the father and husbands of the imprisoned women.

The gendered nature of the recruitment and derecruitment processes is the initial stage at which gendered mobilization occurs. Gender role ideology has been used as an exclusionary tactic as in the cases of Freedom Summer and the anti-pass "bail out" policy. It has also served as an inclusionary recruitment strategy as engaged in by the Federation of South African Women (FSAW). The bottom line is that, depending on the context, movement mobilization is infused with the interactive effect of gender, race/ethnicity, and class that becomes reflected in the composition of the movement and the roles of participants in ongoing recruitment efforts.

Gender Role Differences in Mobilization: Bridging as Leadership

Women and men are often called upon to play differentiated roles in formal movement structures and their recruitment efforts. These gender asymmetries and imbalances that characterize social movement organizations (SMOs) at times mirror the structure of relationships and power differentials between women and men in the larger societal context. The conception of gender-divided labor which assigns women the expressive work of cementing relationships and providing emotional support and gears men toward the instrumental work outside of the family is often mirrored in the structures that facilitate movement mobilization.

In social movements, similar dichotomistic logic is used to describe two categories of participants: leaders and followers. In the dominant understanding of movement processes, the "leaders" are viewed as most important in generating support for social resistance effects and attracting new members. These individuals usually hold titled positions within officially recognized movement organizations which were acquired either through some objective election process or as a result of their "charisma" and/or powerful presence. Much like the male role in the normative family gender split, the leader dominantly represents the movement to the world external to the movement world. The "followers," "masses," or "rank and file" of the movement are conceptualized as the workers who carry out the dictates of the leaders.

In gender-integrated movements, patriarchal assumptions are often superimposed on this hierarchical conception of leadership, creating a gender split in movement roles and leadership patterns. Specifically, this gendered public/private sphere split in social movement roles places men more than women in official leadership positions and relegates most of the women to the more supportive, expressive, and background roles. The "master narrative," or dominant story of the major events in any movement that is passed on to future generations, usually focuses on the activities of official leaders, while the faceless masses, who are disproportionately women, become either invisible or blurred. Contemporary social movement theorists and activists argue for rethinking and conceptualizing the type of leadership that is viewed as most significant in movement mobilizing (Robnett 1997). While official and formally recognized movement organizations often privilege the official leader role in motivating people to join resistance movements, the bridge leaders, a larger proportion of whom are women, are often the actual "foot soldiers" who persuade people to involve themselves in movement efforts.

Both the anti-apartheid and civil rights movements were skewed with respect to the degree to which women and men held leadership positions. The small number of women who held formal titles within official social movement organizations was in no way proportionate to their level of movement participation (Payne 1990). Women very often outnumbered men in these groups, but never possessed equivalent recognized stature with either titled or untitled men in the movement (Robnett 1997). Nonetheless, women wielded significant power in the informal realm and the "cracks and crevices" between organizations and titles. Civil rights movement scholars such as Bernice McNair Barnett, Belinda Robnett, and Charles Payne have consistently argued that women in these undefined and unsupervised areas of the movement were actually the main mobilizers and sustainers (Barnett 1995; Robnett 1996, 1997; Payne 1990; Sachs 1988). In Charles Payne's words, "men led, women organized." Women and their organizations established crucial links between movement structures, various sectors, generations, and ideological persuasions of the "masses." Termed either "invisible leadership," "bridge leadership," or "center women," this work is the essential glue that attracts and holds participation in the movement (Barnett 1995, Robnett 1997; Sachs 1988).

Women's wings and "spin-off" gender-separate organizations emerged as additional mobilization tools that countered barriers against women's mobilization into officially recognized movement organizations. The ANC's Women's League, the Federation of South African Women, and SNCC's Women's Caucus, and the Third World Women's Alliance (established in 1968) are examples of gender-specific bridging structures. Akin to the role of individual female bridge leaders, these autonomous women's organizations played a significant role in bridging between movement organizations. For example, while the male-led ANC, PAC, and BCM were separated in terms of membership, ideology, and ultimate objectives, the FSAW was a coalition of women from a broad range of racial and ethnic backgrounds and organizational affiliations (Walker 1982; Baard 1986). Frances Baard remembers,

> The Federation [of South African Women] was made up of all the organizations that were at the conference: the ANC Women's League, the Congress of Democrats, the South African Indian Congress and the Coloured People's Organization. You could not join the Federation as an individual; you had to be a member of one of those organizations and then you were automatically a member of the Federation. (Baard 1986, 46)

The official movement structures in which men dominated tended to be more dogmatic and separate in their formation, while individual women and autonomous women's organizations in the civil rights movement offered a place for merging the various tendencies and structures of the larger movement.

Interestingly, this crucial work and positioning of women in the movement was due, in part, to the constraints that existed on women's official leadership roles. Excluded from the more elite roles in the movement hierarchy, women were more likely to be the door-to-door canvassers and field workers (Payne 1995). In addition, women were often more willing to take a radical stance and to push further in their demands, since they essentially had more to gain and less to lose from capitulating to the power structures. The greater likelihood that men could parlay their movement roles into "legitimate" positions vested their interests in maintaining cooperative relations with power structures. Women, particularly those from working class or impoverished backgrounds like Fannie Lou Hamer of the civil rights movement and Frances Baard in the anti-apartheid movement, had little incentive to preserve the status quo (Payne 1990; Robnett 1997).

In the case of the U.S. civil rights movement, the period from 1960 to 1965 was characterized by decentralized movement structures that allowed

African American women to play crucial bridge-leading roles regardless of their blocked access to official titles. The Student Nonviolent Coordinating Committee, initiated by a bridge leader of the highest order—Ella Baker—employed a decentralized organizational structure that was amenable to gender egalitarianism and a high level of activism among both women and men. Instrumental in bringing together the student activists that formed the first SNCC membership in 1960, Ella Baker infused the organization with the praxis of "participatory democracy" (James 1999). This philosophy was a reflection of her own style of participation in the movement. In an interview conducted in the late 1970s, Baker explained:

> "I set up the office of the Southern Christian Leadership Conference in 1958, but you didn't see me on television, you didn't see news stories about me. The kind of role that I tried to play was to pick up pieces or put together pieces out of which I hoped organization might come. The theory is, strong people don't need strong leaders." (cited in Cantarow and O'Malley 1980)

As previously explained, Baker's movement biography directly countered the view at the time that male ministers were the sole legitimate "leaders" of the movement.

Such unofficial arena leadership, although devalued and considered relatively unimportant, is often the glue that holds a movement together. What these bridge leaders lacked in status, they made up for in autonomy and impact (Robnett 1997). In an odd gender twist, women with official leadership titles had more constraints on their political role than either their untitled female or titled male counterparts. Titled African American female activists were often more vulnerable to male domination in the office and in assignments than were the more free-lance activists.

The gender ideology and practices of the larger society also play a role in movement mobilization. For instance, one of the rationales given for the predominance of female participation in the U.S. civil rights movement is the "differential reprisal interpretation" (Payne 1990). This concept rationalizes women's high level of activism as the result of less severe reactions from the opposition. Men were potentially perceived as more of a threat and, therefore, targeted more often for their participation. Indeed, while African American women were subject to numerous types of indignities and humiliations, they suffered fewer lynchings in the South and, with some exceptions, were less likely to be subject to direct violence from the FBI and police during the Black Power phase of the movement.

Payne (1990) is suspicious of this explanation, pointing to numerous examples of women being reacted against violently by movement opponents and the tendency for reprisals to be directed at entire families. As has been widely noted, race and class interacted with gender to undermine the applicability of "femininity" to women of African descent. Therefore, from the standpoint of the state's social control, "woman-ness" did not protect women of African descent.

As the movement progressed into the Black Power phase, from 1966 to 1974, and became more masculinized and centralized, the spaces for women's roles as bridge leaders and mobilizers began to close (Giddings 1984; Robnett 1997). The mid-1960s' shift toward the North and away from the voter registration drives and direct actions de-emphasized the grassroots level and left less room for the bridging roles that women had previously played. The Black Panther Party (BPP) promoted a "revolutionary nationalist" philosophy that virtually equated African American liberation with Black male empowerment and masculinist forms of power (Matthews 1998). This perspective posed legitimate African American women's activism as supportive to male dominance in the movement and labeled any stonger type of resistance on the part of women as symbolic castration or a "matriarchal coup d'etat." The more patriarchal nationalistic tendency in this movement relegated women's roles to the background and often called on African tradition as justification (Giddings 1984).

These decentralized structures, characteristic of SNCC in its earlier years, were more conducive to the participation of women than are the hierarchical and centralized social movement structures, which are typically led and dominated by men (McAdam 1992). Once the movement develops in this direction, the spaces within which women's mobilization is generated greatly reduce and even close. The trajectory of the civil rights movement seems to mirror this progression.

In the 1950–59 phase of the anti-apartheid movement, women played important roles in "free spaces" that linked various entities of the movement. In the initial spontaneous mobilizations such as the anti-pass demonstrations and beer raids, the majority of the participants were women. Prior to 1960, women were mobilized mainly through the autonomous women-led structures, such as the Federation of South African Women (FSAW) and the Congress of Mothers, as well as through their informal networks and groupings (Cock 1993; Walker 1982; Wells 1993). The mass quality of the movement changed, though, after the banning of FSAW and the other major liberation organizations in 1960 (e.g., the ANC, PAC, and SAIC). During this severely repressive period, movement organizations and activists were forced to go underground or into exile. At the same time, the military factions of the movement became dominant and the major movement organizations adopted armed struggle as the major form of resistance. The armed guerrilla wing, *Umkhonto we Sizwe* (Spear of the Nation), and POQO, formed by the ANC and PAC, respectively, skewed the gendered participation in the movement toward men. The legislative and military repression during the years between 1960 and 1974 temporarily closed opportunities for women's participation in movement mobilization and other activities.

Informal Kinship and Communication Networks

To this point, we have been concentrating on those networks that are formal and officially recognized. Just as important, if not more so, are those informal networks such as those that flow along kinship lines or are situated in neighborhoods and communities. The kinship and family networks, friendship groupings, and residential or constructed communities comprise an often ignored spectrum of networks through which movement participants are mobilized (Snow, Zurcher, and Ekland-Olson 1980). Emma Mashinini, who would become a prominent South African union organizer in the 1970s and 1980s, says of her own introduction to political struggle,

> I don't know exactly when I became politicised. . . . There were many papers which were going about, and the meeting was clearly advertised, but it was only when my friends approached me that I really took notice of it. (Mashinini 1989, 23)

Mashinini's quote illustrates the importance of informal social networks and lines of communication in bringing individuals into a movement's more formalized structures. Although these mobilizing networks are often devalued in the course of the movement and in movement scholarship in relation to the more formal structures and organizations, they play an important role in galvanizing support for and participation in any movement. According to historian Iris Berger, there is an "ease with which women have come together to voice their demands. . . on a tradition of union organizing but also on a history of women's solidarity expressed in religious organizations, informal assistance networks, [and] community based protest movements" (Berger 1986, 218).

As discussed at the onset of this chapter, the networks and structures that draw people in to protest activities follow the paths of the social relations that characterize their daily lives. That is, movement participation tends to be structured along the locations in which people find themselves:

the workplace, the community, and/or the family. These networks and structures that impact movement mobilization are embedded in the gendered nature of the social order. The centrality of women in household and community spheres affords them greater access to and need for kinship-based and community-centered social networks (Payne 1990). At the same time, the informal neighborhood and grassroots structures through which women have been mobilized are often less visible than the more officially recognized structures (Rodriguez 1994; Schild 1994). In her study of neighborhood organizations in Chili, Veronica Schild found that women played fundamental roles and were highly engaged in "residence-based" struggles which she compared against "production struggles" in which men were disproportionately engaged (Neuhouser 1995; Rodriguez 1994; Schild 1994). Women's greater integration in these social networks is partly due to their greater need for social support in their roles as primary caretaker of the young and the old and as domestic worker (usually in addition to economic provider).

During the anti-apartheid struggle, South African women often joined the struggle through community activities associated with self-help, family security, and community concerns. The "Manyano" collectives that were initially formed in the townships by working- and lower-class African women are examples of informal mobilizing structures in action. These mutual aid collectivities, which originated in church congregations and which organized saving clubs and provided other "welfare" services for women in the townships, were used in service of the movement (Meer 1985). Subsequently, according to scholar-activist Fatima Meer,

> Manyanos . . . converted temporarily into protest groups against apartheid. They defended women's right to brew beer in the 1940s, resisted the extension of passes to women in 1913 and in the 1950s, and agitated against the expropriation of Africa-owned property and forced removals in 1954, as well as against statutory inferiorisation of African education in 1955. (Meer 1985, 14)

The 1959 Cato Manor uprising is another example of the significance of "informal" networks in movement mobilization. Cato Manor, referred to as *Mkhumbane* by its African residents, was an overcrowded and impoverished shantytown near the city of Durban in which many women brewed traditional beer made from malt, sugar, bread, and yeast for income. They also ran and operated *shebeens*—house-based shops or clubs that sold alcoholic drinks (Malahleha 1985). During the latter part of the 1950s, at the same time authorities began to relocate the residents of Cato Manor, the government stepped up enforcement of the legislative prohibitions against making and selling *mqonbothi* and *isishmiyana*, the home brewed beer. In protest against the liquor raids and displacement, more than 3,000 protesters surrounded the beer hall, threatened the men drinking inside with sticks, fought the police, and destroyed beer in official beer halls. The mobilizers used the submerged social networks that were established to avoid police scrutiny of their home-brewing activities to organize the protests. The lack of male involvement in many of these township actions indicates the skewed gender nature of these networks and the overwhelming presence of women in the townships and reserves (Lapchick 1981; Magubane 1979; Nauright 1996). Although the protests were originally directed against the restrictive beer policies, they later expanded to include additional grievances such as pass laws, forced removals, increased taxes, police brutality, and other apartheid practices (Women's International Resource Exchange 1982). The protests reached a zenith in 1960 when protesters attacked and killed nine policemen, one of the incidents which led to the state of emergency declared by the South African government in 1960 (la Hausse 1988).

A similar pattern of the importance of informal and community-based networks like the church is evident in the U.S. civil rights movement of the 1950s and 1960s. In his interviews with female civil rights activists, Charles Payne (1990) found that "when explaining their own decisions to join the movement, . . . respondents constructed answers primarily in terms of either religious belief or preexisting social networks of kinship and friendship" (Payne 1990, 160). Many of the older women who became activists were following the lead of their children. In a movement in which the church formed a central organizing base, the informal interaction among members of the congregations was important in the mobilization process. While male ministers comprised the official leadership, women comprised the majority of church members and supporters in the southern urban church. In fact, women's networks placed pressure on this leadership to take stances that they were not originally inclined to take. E. D. Nixon, an ex-Pullman Porter and NAACP activist in the 1950s, countered the reluctance of the male ministers to overtly support the Montgomery Bus Boycott where he charged,

> "You guys have went around here and lived off of these poor washerwomen all your lives and ain't never done nothing for 'em. And now you got a chance to do something for 'em, you talkin' about you don't want the White folks to know it." (quoted in Giddings 1984, 266)

A gendered social movement analysis appreciates these differences in mobilization paths and structures on the basis of the relative social positioning of women and men. This perspective asserts the crucial role played by informal and submerged networks and communication linkages, those usually devalued from the standard study of social movements. Finally, it forces a "rethinking of movement leadership" and counters the oversimplistic and binary leader/masses dichotomy in favor of a more dynamic and complex understanding of the relationship between movement sectors and mobilizing structures.

Micromobilization:
Grievances, Action Frames, and Identities

In assessing participation in social movements, it is just as necessary (if not more so) to acknowledge the role of intangibles such as inspiration and emotion in persuading individuals to become actively engaged in social movements. In essence, people affected by some social condition worthy of rebellion are merely mobilization potential. In order to activate this potential, they must somehow be "inspired" as opposed to actually engage in movement activities. The question remains as to how, given the same larger structural conditions of inequality and access to organizational resources, some individuals become active in social movements and others do not. In addition to the broad structural and organizational factors in social movement mobilization, individual consciousness and subjectivity is a crucial factor.

The subjective aspect of micromobilization focuses on the motivations, ideologies, and grievances to which potential movement recruits respond (Chaney 1975). Subjectively, an ideological framework that explains the source of the problem and poses a solution to potential movement participants is a necessary component for mobilization. "Grievance models," collective framing, and identity approaches that focus on issues of individual perceptions and consciousness as factors in social movement mobilization operate on the microlevel (Buechler 1993; Johnston, Larana, and Gusfield 1997; Snow et al. 1986; Melucci 1985).

Structurally, the gendered division of labor has an impact on the availability of time and energy that potential activists have to devote to movement activities. On the subjective level, gender ideologies and identities have been drawn on and strategically deployed to stimulate movement participation differentially for women as opposed to men

(Taylor and Whittier 1992). These gender structures and ideologies have to be taken into account for a complete analysis of the micromobilizational factors such as grievances, collective action frames, collective identities, and symbolism in persuading people to become active in social struggle.

Grievances and Collective Action Frames

No society is perfect and meets all of its members' needs. There are differences, though, in the degree to which a society's members are aware of negative societal conditions, perceive them as problematic, and seek to change them. Social movement participation is fueled by grievances and the complaints that its members have about the structures and processes that affect their lives. Just as the impact of particular social problems differs among a population, so does awareness and interpretation, even within a coherent social movement. Many scholars have linked the mobilization of women to socioeconomic and political conditions related to family survival more strongly than the mobilization of men (Lobao 1990; West and Blumberg 1990). Again, this observation reflects gender asymmetries and the gendered public/private split in the wider society. Do women and men have different complaints or interpretations of a given situation? How do grievances that motivate individuals to join resistance struggles differ by gender?

Because of their immediate effect, family and community life disturbances such as rising food prices, dislocations, housing and movement restrictions, inferior education, and transportation were some of the first issues around which women in South Africa organized and mobilized. Their reactions to bread-and-butter issues and actions to counterthreats to their survival have comprised the backbone of resistance actions at the local level. For example, South African women responded with a vengeance to threats to their homes in the squatters' camps outside the urban centers. In the early 1980s, women organized vigils and protests in response to the forced relocation and repeated demolition of the Crossroads squatters' camp outside the urban area of Capetown. Grievances were also couched in notions of gender norms. In the South African anti-pass campaigns, FSAW used the lessening of gender differences from the perspective of the apartheid regime as motivation for involvement. An educational pamphlet distributed by the Transvaal Region FSAW and the African National Congress Women's League (ANCWL) entitled "Danger! Passes Are Being Given

To African Women" urges women to join the movement because: "Women will be handcuffed, jailed, and at the mercy of the police, as men are today under the pass laws" (FSAW n.d. [a]). According to Iris Berger (1986) the combined productive and domestic responsibilities of South African women informed their consciousness in a particular way. As opposed to restricting their involvement, these multiple responsibilities constructed their grievances and stimulated their mobilization.

Scholars and activists have observed that in order for grievances to be a sufficient pull into social movement involvement, they must be "framed" in such a manner as to make the social movement activities, goals, and ideology congruent with the individual or group interest (Snow et al. 1986). This entails the construction of a "collective action frame" that relates to those the movement seeks to organize and recruit (Zald 1996; Snow and Benford 1992). Framing is a necessary condition for social movement participation because it cognitively links the individual to the social movement. The specific "collective action frames" drawn upon by a social movement must link to a "master frame" with which everyone is familiar. An example often cited is the civil rights movement which drew upon the "American" frame of "equality and human rights" to contextualize efforts toward civil rights for people of African descent. As in this example, social movements often extend the society's dominant gender frames to justify and support social action. Gender asymmetries and divisions in the wider society are reflected in the grievances around which movement participants organize.

More obviously, socially defined associations with masculinities and femininities are sometimes explicitly or implicitly embedded in the collective action frames to encourage mobilization. These conceptions of feminine and masculine norms in society and divisions of labor between women and men can limit women and men to particular functions and stations in a movement. As we saw in the case of a motherist frame, they can also be played upon in the justification for movement involvement and the construction of collective identities. Collective identity is an interactive and shared definition produced by several individuals (or groups at a more complex level) and concerned with the orientations of action. By this process of interaction, negotiation and conflict over the definition of the situation, and the movement's reference frame, members construct the collective "we."

Not only do gender roles figure prominently in the construction of collective movement identities, they are also shaped in the process of movement activism. The effects of gender distinctions in society that create differential mobilization can be seen clearly in the aforementioned example of the centrality of motherhood and nurturing for women as an collective identity "draw" into activism. Actions such as FSAW's anti-pass campaign explicitly evoked the roles and responsibilities associated with women as mothers and the primacy of the family. The petition presented to the Prime Minister of South Africa on August 9, 1956, highlighted the potential impact of passes on women's lives (see Appendix 2b):

- That homes will be broken up when women are arrested under pass laws;
- That children will be left uncared for, helpless, and mothers will be torn from the babies for failure to produce a pass;
- That women and young girls will be exposed to humiliation and degradation at the hands of pass-searching police. (FSAW 1956)

Even trade unions and national liberation structures capitalized on the mother role, despite the absence of gender egalitarianism in their structures or policies:

> In contrast to the restrictive constitution of motherhood in the bourgeois ideology, the Congress Alliance and specifically the Food and Canning Workers' Union in the 1950s constructed a "positive, forceful definition of motherhood," which was also collective rather than individualist." (Walker 1995, 422)

Politicized motherhood and motherist movements have been debated with respect to their liberatory prospects (Beall, Hassim, and Todes 1989; Hassim 1993; Walker 1995). Clearly, taking advantage of pre-existing gender role socializations in society benefits the movement. Controversy arises over whether the collective identity as mother, even used for opposition and resistance, further entrenches the subordinate and rigidly defined status of women. As late as 1990, critics were charging the political movements in South Africa with the inability to disentangle "woman" from "mother" in the analyses presented at the Malibongwe conference designed to place gender on the agenda of the negotiations for democratic reforms in the country (Walker 1995; Charman et al. 1991).

As complement to the "naturalization of caring"—the assumed innate propensity for women to engage in nurturing and supportive activities—its correlate male protector and breadwinning role also spills over into movement ideology (Peteet 1989, 1991). The strategic use of this gender role can also serve to stimulate movement involvement. Often, men are encouraged to participate in national liberation struggle by appeals to their masculine role of "protector" (Sharoni 1995b). Both the Black Power phase of the racial/national liberation movement and the armed struggle phase of the anti-apartheid movement played on notions of masculinity, militarism, and patriarchy in their mobilization of African American men.

On the other side of the gender dialectic, these same gender constructs and frames can be constraints to full social movement participation (Lobao 1990). Patriarchies and sexist notions have been cited as major impediments to the mobilization of women into gender-integrated movements. In a 1956 report of the Transvaal Region of the FSAW, "backwards attitudes of men" was listed under the heading of "difficulties and handicaps of the Federation" (FSAW 1956, 3). According to the report:

> Even in the African National Congress and the Indian Congress, many men who are politically active and progressive in outlook still follow the tradition that women should take no part in politics, and a great resentment exists towards women who seek independent activities or even express independent opinions. This prejudice is so strong that even when many of those in leading positions in the ANC appear to be cooperating with the Federation, it is sometimes difficult to avoid the conclusion that they would prefer to hinder the work of the Federation and to withdraw their own women-folk from activities. (FSAW 1955, 3)

Patriarchal attitudes were such a threat to the work of FSAW that it saw fit to publish an article in *Sechaba* (the official ANC publication) the next year titled "Don't Stifle the Work of the Women's Federation." The article insisted that FSAW was "A FULL-BLOODED MEMBER OF THE FREEDOM MOVEMENT AND MUST NOT BE REGARDED—OR TREATED—AS A STEP CHILD" (FSAW 1956).

The Black Power movement also drew on gender ideologies and conceptualizations of the roles of women and men to frame the resistance movement. Specifically, the cultural nationalist philosophy that emerged as a movement belief system in the late 1960s was heavily laden with notions of male dominance and female submission (Fleming 1998; Matthews 1998; Robnett 1997). Generally, this collective framing of the movement linked Black liberation to a "constructed" collective memory of a male-dominated pre-colonial African culture. It was also, in part, a counter discourse to the ways that Black men's authority and power had been destroyed through the historical racist processes and institutions operating in America. This frame posed the reestablishment of patriarchy in the Black community, and in the nation, as the equivalence of African American liberation and equality. The revolutionary Black militant man, usually dressed in black and heavily armed, became central to the symbolism of the Black Panther Party, which was established in 1966 in Oakland, California, and other movement organizations during the Black Power phase of the movement. As Tracey Matthews explains:

> Initially, for the Panthers, as for many other Black groups in this period, the quest for liberation was directly linked to the 'regaining' of Black manhood. This was evident in much of the Party's early language and ideology about gender roles generally, and men's roles in particular. In fact, the Black Panther Party for Self-Defense was an all-male organization at the outset. (Matthews 1998, 278)

In fact, the recruitment literature and rhetoric called on African American men to protect and defend the Black community as "your duty to your women and children, to your mothers and sisters" (Matthews 1998).

As reflected in the theorizing of new social movement theorists, collective identities are not only created in concert with existing roles and personas in the society, they are also constructed and created during the course of a movement. Although the Black Panther Party began as an all-male organization and directed its recruiting efforts toward men, its female recruit membership grew, especially in the late 1960s when the "paramilitary" emphasis of the organization declined (Matthews 1998). The Black Panther Party of the late 1960s was characterized by more explicit discussions of gender roles, increasing numbers of women in titled and untitled leadership positions, and the forging of a new collective identity—the "Black Revolutionary Woman." This persona called on Panther women to be militant and revolutionary, yet at the same time the Black man's "everything."

While Panther women were not very well represented in the titled positions of the organization until Elaine Brown became the first woman to become chairman in 1974, they did play active and important roles in the organization. While the "revolutionary Black Woman role" included support for the "brothers" in the movement (including sexual access, at times), it also absorbed the more masculine and confrontative resistance strategies and roles. Panther women spoke at rallies and meetings, provided analyses and revolutionary analysis for the underground press, went to jail, and were exiled (Foner 1970, 1990; Matthews 1998). While more male activists in the party were killed in their confrontations with the police, activists like Kathleen Cleaver, who was exiled with her husband Eldridge in Algeria, and Assata Shakur, who was jailed and escaped to Cuba, were staunch revolutionaries who devoted their lives to the struggle.

Gendered Mobilization:
A Synthesis of the Macro-, Meso-, and Microlevels

A gendered analysis of social movement mobilization requires scholars to link the multilevels of the struggle and the external environment within or against which it operates. Gender distinctions and divisions lead to different political opportunities for resistance, distinct experiences within movement organizations, and subjective analyses and grievances in the mobilization process.

Although, for the purposes of analysis, we can treat these aspects of mobilization separately in this discussion, they are actually intertwined and interdependent. Structural conditions open different paths to social movement mobilization based on gender. At the same time, at the end of this path gender-differentiated social networks place individuals within separate or parallel movement structures or with distinct roles within those organizations (Nauright 1996; Rodriguez 1994; Robnett 1996, 1997). On the individual level, consciousness and perception of social conditions can vary depending on one's social positioning. Class, race/ethnicity, and cultural factors intersect with these gender processes and structures to configure the paths and levels of mobilization; hierarchies and power dynamics within mobilizing structures; and motivations and stimulus for action.

Whereas early social movement research debated the relative importance of objective/structural versus subjective/ideological factors in stimulating and sustaining social movement activity, more recent work in the field encourages a synthesis between these major approaches. By converging the discussion of structure and ideology, it is possible to explore and appreciate the dialectical relationship between these levels of social struggle and to more clearly view the dynamic social movement process. Using gender as a lens helps to facilitate this type of analysis.

CHAPTER 5

Social Resistance Strategies: The Myth of Gender Neutrality

Pots and pans are so prevalent in women's protests that Kramarae and Treichler (1985, 350) have defined them in their *Feminist Dictionary* as "instruments of protest." (West and Blumberg 1990, 27)

Movement Strategies and Tactics: Gender Blind?

The fact that everyday items such as pots and pans can become instruments of protests is an example of the way gendered processes, as well as women's and men's institutionalized social roles, get incorporated into social movement strategies. For instance, politically conservative Chilean women wielded pots and pans in their 1973 demonstrations against the socialist government led by Salvador Allende, whose reformist policies had improved the quality of life for the poorest of the population but had also resulted in food shortages in the country. In 1985, after the coup d'etat that ousted Allende and installed the repressive military regime of General Pinochet, Allende's female supporters took to the streets with pots and pans (Kaplan 1990). These women's organizations were essentially on opposite ends of the political spectrum, but they similarly used pots and pans in their nonviolent demonstrations to bring attention to their grievances just as women have in a variety of different social struggles around the world. Pots and pans are utensils that are, in many cases, accessible because of, and symbolic of, the domestic labor to which women have been relegated in the gendered division of labor. Likewise, armed warfare can be viewed as an extension of the male role into which men in various societies have been socialized. As a result, armed resistance and military action is usually a male-led social movement strategy.

At the same time, though, these normative gender roles are often undermined and transformed during social movements. Women and men often engage in resistance strategies in ways that challenge and counter their positioning in society. For instance, women have been active fighters in armed struggle and guerrilla warfare, movement strategies that are more associated with men and masculinity. The strategic actions taken by movements are, at times, compatible with normative gender roles, while at other times call for participation that counters the positioning of women and men in the society. At times, gendered identities and roles serve, themselves, as social movement strategy (Sharoni 1995b). West and Blumberg explain:

> Prescribed gender-role behavior in a patriarchal society has provided strategic opportunities for protest. For example, making the most of "saintly" stereotypes, women have used their long skirts to conceal weapons and their "ordinary" households to provide "safe houses" in revolutionary situations. In contrast, drawing on their "temptress" role and sexual resources, they have worked as spies. (West and Blumberg 1990, 27)

These are all expressions of the way in which gender interacts with social movement strategy. They illustrate the fact that the gendered social contexts and the social position of the aggrieved factor into the determination, implementation, and success of social movement strategy.

This chapter focuses on the ways in which societal gender roles, divisions, and power relations are implicated in the strategies and tactics that challengers utilize in social protest movements. How does the gender composition of a movement affect the adoption or rejection of particular strategies? Do societal gender norms and roles influence the tactics that will be used to confront the larger power structures, and who uses them? What about the impact of gender location on the perception and success of particular social movement strategies? I argue in this section that the strategies devised by social resistance movements to bring attention to instances of injustice, mobilize masses of people, and/or transform social systems are influenced by the way gender has been institutionalized and structured into society. This chapter explores these questions concerning the ways gender, as a structured social institution, impacts the development, participation in, perception of, and effect of social movement strategy. It will also make visible some social resistance strategies and actions that have been submerged or hidden as a result of masculinized notions of "legitimate" collective action. I argue that, as opposed to being gender-neutral, the methods used in social struggles are grounded in the gender hierarchies and roles of the society and the movement. These strategies can also transform and impact the way gender is perceived and lived in the transformed society that results.

The Structuring of Social Protest

[T]he expression of defiance is patterned by features of institutional life.
(Piven and Cloward 1979, 15)

The relationship between women, pots, and pans is not a natural phenomenon but one that has been established, in many places, as part of a larger institutionalized system of gender inequality and separation of roles. As the Piven and Cloward observation reminds us, these types of institutionalized social processes and relationships pattern social movement strategy. While social movements pose challenges to established social structures and usually stand outside, and often diametrically opposed to, the legitimate political processes, they also reflect aspects of these social structures. Even though movement strategies and tactics often appear spontaneous and have an aura of immediacy, they are very much structured by and grounded in the concrete social context and subjective interpretations of both the movement and the wider society (Piven and Cloward 1979; Tarrow 1995; Tilly 1986). In other words, movement organizations and activists always operate within a particular context of constraints and opportunities with regard to the types of actions that are available and that they adopt. The methods of resistance that are subsequently used express a balance of forces between the social environment and actual movement conditions (Minkoff 1993). Minkoff identified three main factors that play heavily in the choice of movement actions: organizational characteristics, environmental conditions, and strategic choices made by movement participants, leaders, and organizations.

Social movement strategies can be differentiated between those that are geared toward mobilizing resources and building the movement internally—e.g., raising money and providing shelter—and those that are directed at external targets. The width of the range of strategies and tactics employed by a movement is its "tactical flexibility." In some instances, social movements borrow strategies and tactics used by previous struggles to create what scholars have labeled a "spillover effect." In other cases, new forms of protest are generated or previously utilized methods are combined in different ways, leading to what has been termed "tactical innovation." Methods and strategies of resistance have been additionally categorized on the basis of numerous criteria including their level of spontaneity/organization, their use of force or violence, and the amount of risk involved. Tarrow's (1995) classification, for example, rests on the relative level of "contentiousness" that a strategy displays. He characterizes movement actions as either the politics of order, the politics of disorder, or the politics of violence. The "politics of order" includes nonviolent and restrained ways to bring about change such as legal actions, boycotts, and petitions. In contrast, strategies that entail mild confrontation such as direct action campaigns, demonstrations, and occupations are considered the "politics of disorder." Finally, the "politics of violence" includes direct aggression on the part of movement participants as they engage in forced entries, violent attacks, and/or acts of sabotage. In any given phase of a social movement, while strategies may be utilized on all of these levels, there is usually a dominant approach.

The politics of gender is also embedded in social movement strategy. To the extent that institutionalized differences exist between women and men and determine social location in a society, the opportunities for defiance is also gender structured (Piven and Cloward 1979; McAdam 1992; Robnett 1997). Social positioning on the basis of gender determines the concrete settings within which movement participants experience their deprivation, perceptions of group identities, and institutionalized roles, as well as the particular strategic approaches that flow from these relationships at any point in the movement (Noonan 1995). For instance, working as a domestic servant does not lend itself to a strike in the same way that being a factory worker does. On the other hand, a strike is not an appropriate or effective action at the community level for forestalling demolition or getting needed services. As far as social change strategies, people work with what they have, from where they are stationed, to accomplish specific objectives.

The significance of gender as a factor in social movement strategies is evident in interrelated ways. First, distinctions between women and men in their social roles, both personal and public, impact the available strategies that they adopt when they are the dominant participants in a movement structure. Secondly, the dominant strategic approach that characterizes a movement during a particular period is often differentially accessible to women and men. This differential access could have either structural or ideological roots. Finally, some acts of resistance have been made virtually invisible due to the male-biased notion of appropriate, legitimate, and/or valued forms of collective action.

Gender Symmetry and Asymmetry in Resistance Strategies

"Cycles of protest" are distinct periods within a social movement that are characterized by a particular range of protest forms or "repertoires of contention." The cycle itself consists of

> an increasing and then decreasing wave of interrelated collective actions and reactions to them whose aggregate frequency, intensity, and forms increase and then decline in rough chronological proximity. (Tarrow 1995, 95)

While any given protest cycle may include a variety of strategies and tactics being used either simultaneously or in tandem, there are usually dominant forms of protest employed during each period. For each cycle, there are those "established means of popular protest that are known and regarded as legitimate within a given social milieu" (McAdam and Snow 1997, 326). At the same time that particular strategies come to be dominant, new protest tactics are continually being developed as the contenders transform themselves in response to the constraints and opportunities provided by the external environment. This process, considered "tactical innovation," is affected by the gender dynamics both internal and external to the movement.

A major theme of this chapter is that forms of resistance do not magically appear, but are structured and created through the dynamic interplay between key factors in the social environment and the movement, including gender (McAdam 1983; Piven and Cloward 1977; Tarrow 1994). A gender lens helps to identify the ways the "established" and emerging resistance strategies and actions are mediated by gendered hierarchies and assumptions. Some social movement strategies are asymmetrical with respect to gender participation and/or roles. In gender-asymmetric social movement strategies there is skewed access to or involvement in particular social movement activities. That is, some strategies used to consolidate movements, pressure elites, and/or transform social structures are more "gender friendly," so to speak, than others. Generally speaking, strategies that reflect the "politics of order" and "disorder" lend themselves to similar levels and types of participation on the parts of both women and men. This includes actions ranging from petitioning and staging sit-ins, to participating in demonstrations and civil disobedience.

In contrast, some social movement strategies are more vested in gender assumptions and/or tied to gender-differentiated institutions. Social resistance strategies such as burning draft cards, which was employed in the U.S. anti-war protests of the 1960s, or demonstrating as mothers in search of disappeared loved ones, as engaged in by motherist organizations in South Africa, Chile, and El Salvador, are characterized by gender-skewed accessibility. In both the anti-apartheid and civil rights movements, there were periods in which women and men had differential relationships to, and inclusion in, the strategies that were adopted to counter the power structures. In general, the more mass or large-scale the strategic approach, the more gender accessible. In addition to the gendered continuum of relative accessibility and validation of activities, patriarchal bias in our understanding of social resistance has rendered many strategies unnoticed and unappreciated.

Symmetrical Movement Strategies

During the cycles of protest that characterized the U.S. civil rights and South African anti-apartheid movements, the strategies and tactics used to confront the established power structures embodied gender in particular ways. Mass "nonviolence" and civil disobedience characterized the early phases of the national/racial liberation movements in both the United States and South Africa. "Boycotts, strikes, mass marches or demonstrations, and planned civil disobedience are all forms of nonviolent resistance" (Fredrickson 1995, 225). These types of strategies allowed for participation of both women and men, although roles were often differentiated. Very often, the female impact in certain types of boycotts was more pronounced due, in great part, to the consumer role played by women in the domestic unit. Domestic responsibilities placed them in more powerful positions vis-à-vis men in withholding patronage. Boycotts, protests, and collective noncompliance were accessible by both women and men because they did not dictate any specific gender role for participation.

The Montgomery Bus Boycott of 1955 set off a wave of successful nonviolent protest actions that occurred in the United States. Between 1955 and 1965 the racial/national liberation movement activity in the United States consisted mostly of boycotts, sit-ins, mass arrests, and freedom rides as forms of civil disobedience, and community-wide protest campaigns (McAdam 1983). These strategies were dependent on mass support and high levels of commitment and participation on the part of activists. Both women and men were intricately involved in these efforts at various stages and different levels, depending on the sites of the activities. Churches and student organizations, which were comprised of high levels of female membership and male official leadership, provided the base of support for the movement (McAdam 1982; Morris 1984; Payne 1995). The "Freedom Rides" initiated by the Congress on Racial Equality (CORE) in 1961 is an example of a strategy in which women and men were equally involved. In the Freedom Rides, African Americans and European Americans tested the compliance of the southern states with the Supreme Court's rulings against racial segregation by riding buses together from the North to the South. After the first wave of riders was attacked by local "White mobs" in Anniston, Alabama, the riders were flown out of Alabama in order to regroup. Convinced of the importance for this resistance work to continue, Diane Nash and Ruby Doris Smith volunteered themselves and other members of the Nashville chapter of the Student Nonviolent Coordinating Committee to continue the rides from Birmingham, Alabama. These two women, who had been extremely active in the sit-ins and demonstrations up to that point, were able to persuade James Farmer, the head of CORE, to agree. They proceeded to raise money for transportation and organize other students to engage in the second wave of the Freedom Rides which eventually ended with arrests in Jackson, Mississippi.

The struggle in South Africa between 1950 and 1959 also used nonviolent, yet confrontational, strategic actions against the institutionalized power structure that required mass mobilization (Taylor 1997; Walker 1982). These collective actions included mass marches and protests, economic and social boycotts, and noncompliance with unjust and racially discriminatory laws (Baard 1986; Magubane 1979; Taylor 1997; Walker 1982). The largest actions, such as the women's anti-pass marches of 1955 and 1956 and the Congress of the People (1955), were dependent on massive grassroots canvassing. "Plans for a major event were often preceded by a build-up of smaller localised activities and mini-events, which were part of a process of mobilisation" (Taylor 1997, 76). There were boycotts of bus service against increased fares (Alexandra township, 1957), buying potatoes which were picked with prison labor (1958), and municipal beer halls that undermined women's home-brewing enterprises (Natal 1959). One very successful boycott that drew both women and men into action was the Potato Boycott of the late 1950s. The boycott was organized in opposition to the practice on the part of the South African police of placing young male pass law offenders on potato farms where they would be forced to dig for potatoes with their hands. As Frances Baard put it in her memoirs, "after a time we thought no, if they are going to do this to our children then we must not eat potatoes; we must stop eating the potatoes that are hurting our children so much" (Baard 1986). The boycotters spread the word that the potatoes were "filled with the blood of African people" and were so successful that even workers at the markets refused to carry the potatoes. Once the farmers felt the brunt, they ended the practice of using pass violators as labor on prison farms.

Even in situations that conflicted with gender role norms, such as going to jail, which would ordinarily be incompatible with the notion of "female-ness," the role was expanded to include broad participation. These instances of role transformation can either arise out of necessity or emerge as conscious strategy. The "jail, no bail" strategy was a gender-symmetrical tactic that was used in both the South African and U.S. movements during the 1950s and 1960s. This strategy consisted of mass engagement in civil disobedience through the violation of unjust laws and subsequent refusal of bail. In South Africa, more than 2,000 women were arrested and refused bail during the 1958 anti-pass protests in the townships of Alexandra and Shophiatown (Walker 1982). Of the first activists to utilize the strategy in the United States, the "Rock Hill Four," who were jailed in South Carolina in 1961 for demonstrating against racial segregation, two were women—Ruby Doris Smith and Diane Nash (Evans 1979; Fleming 1998; Giddings 1984; Zinn 1964). Later, when Diane Nash was arrested while pregnant and still refused bail, she responded, "This will be a Black boy born in Mississippi, and thus where ever he is born he will be in prison" (cited in Evans 1979, 40). Mass demonstrations, strikes, vigils, boycotts, sit-ins, protest funerals, and petitions are all on the symmetry side of the gendered strategy continuum (Ackerman and Kruegler 1994; Lofland 1996).

Asymmetrical Movement Strategies

As both the civil rights and anti-apartheid movements progressed, changes in the dominant strategies of the movements in the face of external conditions widened the gender gap, but in particular ways. In both cases, strategic shifts in the movements during the 1960s increased the gender asymmetry movement strategy. Specifically, there was lessened accessibility for women to engage in the more visible resistance strategies of the period. The changes in movement strategy coupled with the divergent conditions in South Africa and the United States offered different opportunities for women to develop alternative strategic approaches within the movement.

Part of the impetus for the shift in movement strategy was the response to movement activities and organizations that came from external forces such as the government and police. In the case of the civil rights movement, legislative reforms in the form of the Civil Rights Act of 1964 were offset by the rise in repression on the part of southern law enforcement and White citizen councils. In South Africa, the nonviolent strategies were confronted with police repression and increased legislative racial oppression in South Africa. Fredrickson points out that

> Militant non-violence was apparently demonstrating its utility in one case and its futility in the other. The American and South African struggles seem to have diverged decisively . . . [with] the coming of the rigorous and oppressive apartheid regime at the same time that civil rights for blacks became a mainstream political issue in the United States. (Fredrickson 1995, 265)

A major strategic shift in social movement strategy in the South African case occurred in 1960 after the violent response of the South African defense forces to the Pan-Africanist Congress-organized Sharpeville protest. The Pan-Africanist Congress of Azania (PAC) was a liberation organization that formed from a split from the African National Congress (ANC) in April 1959. As opposed to the concentration that the ANC placed on multiracialism, the PAC was more nationalistic and concerned more with the liberation and self-determination of the indigenous African people of South Africa. In March 1960, on the heels of the FSAW-led anti-pass campaign, the PAC organized the Anti-pass Positive Action Campaign in which Africans (mostly men) were asked to leave their passes and present themselves to the nearest police station for arrest (Mafole 1995). At Sharpeville approximately 20,000 protesters demonstrated at the police station and were indiscriminately fired on by the police. In what would be called the Sharpeville massacre, more that 79 women, men, and children were killed and 179 injured. In the aftermath of this "crack down" on the movement, the major liberation organizations were "banned" or made illegal in 1960, and a state of emergency which expanded the powers of the state and police was declared in 1962. These developments changed the social and political environment in which the liberation movement operated. As activist Viviene Taylor observed, after the Sharpeville massacre . . . politicization took place in forms other than mass mobilization. There was an intensification of politicization through "underground" or covert study and cell groups. (Taylor 1997, 83)

The adoption of armed struggle and guerrilla warfare by the liberation organizations fueled the creation of armed wings of the ANC in 1961, *Umkhonto We Sizwe* (Spear of the Nation), and the Pan-Africanist Congress, POQO, and marked a strategic shift in the movement. This shift toward the dominance of more military strategies in this movement cycle impacted the relative accessibility and roles played by women and men in the movement. While women participated in the guerrilla activities, their inclusion in this more masculinized and clandestine strategic approach was lower due to cultural prescriptions associated with gender and their relative structural availability. Guerrilla warfare was not only physically dangerous and taxing, it called for longer periods away from home and children. Women's productive and reproductive responsibilities mitigated against extensive participation.

In the case of the civil rights movement, activists found the liberal governmental reforms and legislative efforts such as the desegregation laws and Voting Rights Act of 1964 virtually ineffective. Even in the face of these reforms, peaceful activists continued to be restricted from voting by the local election boards and exposed to violence from White racist opposition groups like the Ku Klux Klan and White citizen's councils without protection from the federal government. Additionally, disillusionment and disappointment followed the nonviolent efforts to democratize the political process that characterized the formation of the Mississippi Freedom Democratic Party (MFDP). The MFDP was coordinated by the Student Nonviolent Coordinating Committee and the Council of Federated Organizations (COFO), formed by SNCC organizers in 1964 as an alternative to the racially exclusive, yet official, Democratic Party (Carson 1981; Robnett 1997). It ran elections for candidates to serve as delegates for the National Democratic Convention, many of whom were women, in which both African Americans and Whites voted. The delegates were "slapped in the face" at the actual convention, which was held that same year in Atlantic City, New Jersey. Instead of seating the MFDP full delegation, a subcommittee of the Credentials Committee offered the MFDP a compromise of two seats; many of the delegates, particularly Fannie Lou Hamer and the other women, vehemently opposed the offer. They persuaded the other delegates to resist the efforts on the part of convention officials and other civil rights leaders to reject the compromise, as well. Hamer, who had testified to convention members to the beatings and humiliations that she had suffered as a result of attempting to vote, was joined by "the other women leaders, holding 'guest' tickets to the convention" and they "forced their way onto the convention floor" (Robnett 1997, 161). The failure of these nonviolent, and gender inclusive, strategies to exact the desired changes led to shifts toward more militancy, as well as racial and gender exclusion, in movement activities.

After the experience of the MFDP in Atlantic City, and the seemingly diminishing returns of the nonviolent mass strategies, a segment of movement activists moved toward more confrontational and vanguard approaches to gaining rights for African Americans. The turn away from nonviolence as the dominant movement strategy, toward more hierarchical organizational structures, and greater gender asymmetry has been marked by the well-known 1964 SNCC meeting held in Waveland, Mississippi (Fleming 1998; Robnett 1997). At this meeting, tensions over the role of Whites in the movement, the roles of women, and the utility of nonviolent strategies reached an all-time high. An anonymously produced position paper on the sexist treatment of women in SNCC, which likened the position of women in SNCC to that of African Americans in a racist society, was presented for discussion.

Although previous SNCC activists acknowledge that some gender discrimination in the organization did exist, its structure and strategies were generally much more open to female leadership and gender egalitarianism than many other movement structures of the period. The gender restrictions that did exist were experienced differently by race and ethnicity. In the area of work assignments, White female SNCC workers were more restricted than their African American counterparts. Later, this paper would be attributed to Mary King and Casey Hayden, two White SNCC workers, thereby also implicating the racial strains that had come to exist in the movement, generally, and specifically between women of African and European American descent. Some of this differentiation was due to the potential danger to all movement workers that accompanied interracial activities (especially when it involved women and men working together) in the extremely racist context of the U.S. South. As a result, White female SNCC workers were more likely to get clerical and office assignments as opposed to many of the African American women who were field workers and had more autonomy.

By 1965, these racial, gender, and class issues came to a head. The purging of White activists from SNCC and the emergence of organizations like the Black Panther Party (established in 1966) ushered in the more militant and nationalist Black Power phase of the movement (Robnett 1997; Perkins 2000). Not only was the White power structure viewed as problematic, the power of women within the movement also became interpreted by some as an impediment to racial emancipation. More quasimilitary and masculinized strategies adopted by groups like the Black Panther Party (BPP) for Self Defense and the Black Liberation Army (BLA) changed the gendered interpretation of, and participation in, movement strategy. According to Elaine Browne, member and later chairman of the Black Panthers,

> A woman in the Black Power movement was considered, at best, irrelevant. A woman asserting herself was a pariah. A woman attempting the role of leadership was, to my proud black Brothers, making an alliance with the "counter-revolutionary, man-hating, lesbian, feminist white bitches." It was a violation of some Black Power principle that was left undefined. If a black woman assumed a role of leadership, she was said to be eroding black manhood, to be hindering the progress of the black race. She was an enemy of black people. (Brown 1992, 357)

Gender asymmetry grew as the dominant movement tactics moved away from the politics of disorder to the politics of violence.

> With the corresponding shift in philosophy and organization, the position of Black women in the struggle for equality and justice took an unprecedented turn. Never before had Black women been required to "step back." (Richardson 1997, 183)

At the same time, activists during the Black Power phase of the movement in the United States consciously transformed and expanded the gender role expectations as a movement strategy. The women in the Black Panther Party (BPP) adopted masculinized symbolism associated with militancy and armed defense. The image of a woman, in black, holding a rifle was, in some ways, even more oppositional to the established order since it conflicted with both the norms of African American complicity with the U.S. power structure and the normative ideology of femininity. Despite this extension of "masculinized" attributes to women in the BPP, certain strategies, such as confronting police when they stopped community residents, were reserved for male members. In addition, the "survival programs" in which more Panther women were engaged were less emphasized and valued. These programs provided free food, clothing, legal assistance, and preventive health care services in various BPP chapters. The first and most popular of these programs was the Free Breakfast for School Children Program, established in 1970, which provided breakfasts for children in the community with food donated by local merchants.

These strategic shifts in the South African and U.S. cases shifted the movements toward more gender asymmetry. Increasingly, participation was closed off in the dominant strategies of the protest cycle, forcing women to pursue alternative and autonomous modes of resistance. Because many of these strategies did not conform to the dominant view of social movement strategies, they remained hidden and submerged.

Submerged and Hidden Strategies:
Women's Political Cultures

Movements are often defined and remembered by the most visible movement strategies and actions, that is, those types of confrontation that receive the most media and scholarly attention. The "master narrative" of a movement usually rests on these movement expressions to officially define and characterize the movement in our collective memories. For example, the civil rights movement has come to be known as a series of sit-ins, boycotts, and demonstrations. The Black Power movement is best known through the Black Panther Party's violent confrontations and shoot-outs with local police departments. In a similar vein, the anti-apartheid movement has become equated with township rebellions and guerrilla warfare on the part of the liberation organizations' military wings. Many of the strategic actions that essentially sustained these movements have slipped through the cracks and been lost to our understandings of resistance strategies.

Recently, scholars and activists have begun to document the more subtle and everyday forms of resistance that are continuously used by oppressed people to challenge actual and/or perceived injustice from established authority structures (Kelly 1994; Scott 1985). These less organized or coordinated forms of resistance to hegemonic power include everything from work slow-downs and noncompliance, to stealing and sabotage. Because of the gendered divisions in many societies and movements, some of the resistance strategies engaged in by women as an outgrowth of their productive and reproductive labor are the very ones that are submerged and hidden. The vital contribution of these less visible strategies to revolutionary and resistance movements is not always obvious and, consequently, have been often neglected and devalued.

Pamela McAllister (1991) has identified several types of resistance action engaged in by women that often get overlooked in our assessments of social movements: sojourning—marches and walks to protest injustices; huggers, sleepers and breastfeeders—refusing to move, confrontation through sit-ins, lie-ins, sleep-ins, die-ins, and breastfeed-ins; strikes—stoppages of productive and reproductive/sexual labor; Mothers' Days and Peace Conferences—International Women's Days; invasions—disruption of governmental bodies and men's proceedings to voice grievances where their voices are not welcome; providing shelter and support; occupations; and using bodies as battlefields—wielding hair, faces, bodies, and feet. Added to this list should be education and cultural expression as resistance strategies in which women have played an active role but are often placed on the back burner (Reagon 1993). The provision of housing and shelter, promotion of liberation education, and development of oppositional culture were all submerged strategies in the civil rights/Black Power and anti-apartheid movements.

Housing and Shelter as Resistance

Providing shelter and refuge, considered an extension of women's nurturing role, is rarely seen as a social resistance strategy. The Crossroads resistance waged by South African women outside of Capetown discussed in chapter 4 is a good example of providing shelter and "refusal to move" as movement strategy. South African women were driven to counter the apartheid regime in this particular way due to their social marginality in the labor force and housing opportunities in South African urban areas. Their predominance in the "illegal" squatters' camps outskirting urban centers provided opportunities for specific types of resistance in the 1970s. The very act of their constructing housing and settling illegally in areas that were forbidden was in noncompliance with apartheid policy and, therefore, an inherently confrontational movement strategy. In addition to "squatting" as a resistance activity, the women of Crossroads utilized a wide range of activities to resist the proposed demolition. They organized twenty-four-hour vigils in an effort to forestall the destruction of their dwellings and maintain the dwellings that they had constructed. Their ultimate show of resistance was sitting in front of the bulldozers slated to destroy the community (Lapchick and Urdang 1982; Landis 1982; Bernstein 1985).

Not only was providing shelter to individuals and families a resistance strategy during the anti-apartheid struggle, providing physical space and shelter to official movement organizations was also necessary due to the clandestine nature of the anti-apartheid struggle. Frances Baard, an organizer with the African National Congress, Federation of South African Women, and labor unions, was one of many movement participants who lent their homes as meeting places for the movement. According to Baard:

> Soon after I joined the ANC they asked me if they could have meetings at my house. Then somebody, either from Capetown or one of the local people, would come and talk to us. They used to teach us about political issues and how to organize people better. . . . When we wanted to organize the women too we would call them to our houses in the evening when they had come back from work. (Baard 1986, 36)

Individual women and women's structures within larger movements also became responsible for fulfilling this housing role during major movement activities. The Federation of South African Women (FSAW) and the ANC Women's League were responsible for organizing shelter for delegates to the 1955 Congress of the People. As an FSAW report documents,

> Together with the African National Congress Women's League, the Federation organised accommodation for 2,000 delegates, the Transvaal secretary travelling from township to township, speaking to large numbers of women, both individually and collectively. (FSAW 1955, 2)

African American women during the civil rights movement also played this role. The movement "mamas" became known for their provision of shelter to voter registration volunteers during Freedom Summer. In Zinn's history of SNCC,

> Negro women in town often became mothers to the SNCC youngsters far from home and family; they put them up, make meals for them, tend them when they are sick, go out on the line with them in demonstrations. (Zinn 1964, 12)

Along the same lines, Evans (1979) quotes activist Charles Sherrod in saying "there is always a 'mama'" (Evans 1979, 51). The "mamas" of the movement, and their provision of political involvement and nurturance, were indispensable to sustaining the movement. According to SNCC member Fran Beal,

The person who cooks, the person who feeds, the person who types, the person who answers the phone, the person who writes out the checks, these roles are very devalued and women play these roles in our society. . . . People just don't write about these roles. But if you ever try to put together an organization or struggle without the people who function in these roles, you won't get very far in your attempt. (Reagon 1979, 42)

These submerged and invisible strategies are the very ones on which other movement activities rest.

Education as Liberation

Providing education and information that expands mass consciousness is another major sphere of resistance activity that is often overlooked and underestimated for its subversive potential. This is true despite the imperative for mass political consciousness for successful movement building. At some point in both the civil rights and anti-apartheid movement, "public" or state-run educational institutions were boycotted and substituted with alternative schools or educational programs (Baard 1986; Brown 1990; LeBlanc-Ernest 1998). Although both men and women participated in these consciousness-raising efforts, this movement strategy was particularly accessible to and staffed by women. Educating and teaching are also more associated with women and the feminine role in these societies.

During the ANC-organized Bantu Education Boycott in 1954–55, African children were taken from the inferior schools run by the government and taught by community activists in "culture clubs" or "education shebeens." A 1955 article in *The Drum* reported the following raid on one of the culture clubs and the militancy on the part of one of the female instructors:

When it was the turn for the children to give their names and addresses, Beauty Moroane ordered them not to comply with the wishes of the police, leading them in Congress slogan songs and doing the Africa sign. The children also made the sign. . . . Beauty was then bundled into the van. (Lunn 1983, 128)

These culture clubs were very similar to the freedom and citizen schools that operated at the Highlander Institute in the southern United States during the early 1960s. In 1962, for example, during a SNCC campaign in Jackson, Mississippi:

Diane Bevel Nash was tried . . . for teaching the techniques of nonviolence to Negro Youngsters; the charge was "contributing to the delinquency of minors" and she was sentenced to two years in jail. (Zinn 1964, 80)

Women like Diane Nash, Septima Clark, and Ella Baker were instrumental in developing the liberation education associated with the voter registration drives during the civil rights movement (Clark 1986; Grant 1998; Zinn 1964).

Septima Clark's role in using education as resistance is particularly noteworthy. After losing her job as a teacher in 1954 as a result of her NAACP membership, Clark was asked to become the director of workshops at Highlander Folk School in Monteagle, Tennessee. The Highlander Folk School was established in 1932 by Myles Horton as a place for people and organizations to discuss and strategize around the problems in their communities. According to sociologist Aldon Morris (1984), movement "halfway houses" such as Highlander were crucial sites for nurturing resistance and sharing strategic information in the resistance struggle. The "citizen education program," directed and taught by Clark, educated African American participants in both general and political literacy. Septima Clark, along with her cousin Bernice Robinson, would first teach participants how to read and write and then present them with information on election laws and the U.S. Constitution in preparation for them to register to vote. Clark and Robinson's participatory teaching strategy was highly successful and is credited with aiding thousands of African Americans to register to vote in the 1950s. Later, in the late 1960s, the Black Panther Party organized alternative schools such as the Oakland Community School (LeBlanc-Ernest 1998). As the male Black Panthers patrolled the streets and intervened between the community and the police, the women organized a Free Breakfast program for the community children and, at the same time, fed them the political position of the party.

Political education and consciousness raising was a major strategy of autonomous/parallel women's organizations. During 1956 alone, the Transvaal region of the Federation of South African Women and the ANCWL could boast of distributing "5,000 printed leaflets on the dangers of passes, . . . 8,000 copies of the pamphlet 'Women in Chains' in English and 5,000 in Sesuto" (FSAW 1956, 3). This twelve-page pamphlet detailed the dangers and potential problems with the issuance of passes for African women. It revealed the government's motives, charged that they would further destroy the family, and evoked the image of "women in handcuffs" to motivate women to join the movement. The pamphlet ends by stating that "women are not afraid of suffering for the sake of their children and their homes" (FSAW 1956, 12).

Creating Oppositional Culture

Even cultural expressions and art take on political significance in the context of a liberation struggle. New social movement theories place greater emphasis on the significance of culture and symbolism, collective identity, and ideology in the process of collective resistance efforts (Melucci 1985; Taylor and Whittier 1992). Culture, the dynamic expression of a people's or social group's way of live, is viewed as a fertile and vibrant site for the production and promotion of opposition and resistance. Culture is dialectical, in a sense, in that, depending on the conditions, it is accessible to the forces that facilitate both oppression and liberation. The creation of oppositional cultural forms is a social movement strategy that works in tandem with, and assists the impact of, other forms of activism. In fact, the very maintenance of a particular "way of life" in face of attempted cultural genocide and assimilation is, in and of itself, resistance. Stella Dadzie identified this practice among African slaves in the West Indies. She found that "African-born and Creole women were able to preserve and pass on to their children a set of values and beliefs, rituals and practices that enable them to resist the degradations of slavery and continue to know their own worth" (Dadzie 1990, 37). These cultural forms of struggle have been and still are essential in movements for national independence and racial equality, as illustrated in the civil rights and anti-apartheid cases. Historically, African and African diasporan women have been prominent at those sites of the production of oppositional culture.

During the civil rights struggle, Fannie Lou Hamer and the Freedom Singers (three of four of whom were women) were known for the inspiration that their songs provided to the participants in direct action campaigns. Zinn (1964) writes what he termed the "new abolitionists" of the civil rights movement,

> Most often, however, they sing. This was true of the farmer and labor movements of this country. . . . They have created a new gospel music out of the old, made up songs adapted or written in jail or on the picket line. Every battle station in the Deep South now has its Freedom Chorus, and the mass meetings there end with everyone standing, led by the youngsters of SNCC, linking arms, and singing "We Shall Overcome." (Zinn 1964, 4)

Bernice Johnson Reagon, an activist in the Albany Movement in 1961 and member of the SNCC Freedom Singers, described women like Fannie Lou Hamer who used song and parable to mobilize social resistance, as "cultural carriers" (Reagon 1993). Reagon went on to establish "Sweet Honey in the Rock," an a capella singing collective in which women of African descent continue the legacy of using song and performance to resist the conditions of social oppression.

The production and sale of the traditional homemade beer was essentially a method of cultural resistance used by South African women. Since, according to apartheid law, South African men were only allowed to consume alcohol in municipal beer halls, the creation and sale of this home brew was, in and of itself, a protest and resistance strategy (Lapchick and Urdang 1982). The struggle of women to maintain this small bit of traditional culture and independence was decidedly anticolonial activity. Many of the protests during the early phase of the anti-apartheid movement that originated against the beer policies expanded to include additional grievances. There was a snowballing effect from this seemingly small area of resistance engaged in by women. For instance, one analyst asserted that the reasons behind the Cato Manor uprising in Natal were poor living conditions, and general poverty, and the flashpoint came with exhaustive beer raids on illegal stills. When the women's grievances were published, they went far beyond the beer halls to include dipping tanks, betterment schemes, increased taxes, influx control, and police provocation (Women's International Resource Exchange 1982, 15).

Silence as Resistance Strategy

Usually, the idea of social protest is equivalent with disruption or "making noise." As a result, the silences that contribute to contestation and resistance are ignored. Aggression and noise can be considered a masculine strategy. There can be just as much resistance and confrontation in silence. Kaplan (1990) identifies silence as an important strategy in women's political culture. This was the case in the sojourning of women in protest to pass laws in South Africa. When the Pretoria City Council banned the 1955 anti-pass march organized by the Federation of South African Women, the women came in silence to present their signed statements of protest to the prime minister. The day proceeded in the following manner:

[N]early two thousand [women] had handed in their signed protests outside the Union Buildings and were seated in the amphitheater in self-deter-
mined silence. Throughout that historic day, no instructions were given; the
women made their protest in their own way, . . . and the two thousand
women sat in silence until they rose to their feet and sang *Nkosi Sikelela Afrika*
as it surely has never been sung before. (Joseph 1956, 3–4)

This action, which left a lasting impact on the South African liberation
struggle, is testimony to the power of silence and cultural opposition in
resistance. Nina Shapiro-Perl found this to also be true in her study of
women workers in a U.S. jewelry factory. She found that the women, who
had been perceived as

the passive and apathetic group, were already engaged in a silent struggle
with management over control of the work process, and that viewing worker
fight-back only in terms of conventional measure of militancy like strikes
or walkouts results in overlooking the more informal but on-going fight-back
strategies that are enduring and creative. (Shapiro-Perl 1984, 194)

When these hidden and submerged forms of resistance are exposed and
appreciated for their interaction with other, more overt, movement strategies, our ideas about activism change.

Beyond the Myth of Gender Neutral Strategy

As many of the examples have illustrated, the strategic approaches that
social movements adopt are grounded in the social context. This context
includes the structure of gender relations as well as the ideologies that pre-
scribe roles for women and men in the society. Not only are social movement
strategies far from gender neutral, they sometimes utilize gender strategically to achieve both internal and external objectives. This was clearly the
case in the "Call for Mothers" to join the anti-pass campaign in South Africa.

At any given time in the life of a social movement, the dominant strategic approach may offer differential access for participation on the parts
of women and men. Further, based on gender bias in the way that resistance is conceptualized, there are often undervalued and invisible strategies
that contribute to social movement success. For instance, while both the
anti-apartheid and civil rights/Black Power movements are referenced by
key moments of overt struggle, there are often "hidden transcripts" of re-

sistance that are just as, if not more, important to sustaining the movement (Scott 1995; Shapiro-Perl 1984). These submerged layers of struggle are often the realm of women, especially during periods of gender asymmetry when the dominant movement strategies exclude or underutilize women's efforts. According to Temma Kaplan,

> examining the action of women engaged in grassroots struggle organized around the pressures of every day life, it is possible to reveal a political tendency whose force and frequency seems to increase with each year. . . . such resistance movements had the potential for creating entirely new egalitarian, democratic organizations. (Kaplan 1990, 259)

Since gender is not fixed or static, it is also transformed through the strategic choices made by social movements and by individuals within those movements. For an instant, near the end of the anti-pass phase of South Africa's anti-apartheid movement, for example, women's heightened political activity increased men's domestic responsibilities. At the same time that women packed the jails, men were left to care for the children and the household (Walker 1982; Wells 1993). In addition to supplying the majority of the household productive labor, many of these women were also the primary "breadwinners." The decision for the men of the ANC to override the women's determination to pack the jails was partially a rejection of their gender role expansion. According to Wells (1993),

> Many ANC men felt the impact of the women's imprisonment quite personally as most of their own wives were involved. . . . Clearly factors of race and traditional gender roles intertwined to play a key role in the eventual decision to bail out the arrested women. (Wells 1993, 121–22)

These transformations in gendered identities may remain after the life of the movement depending on the structure of the society that follows. Alternately, women's participation in strategies that are outside of the typical definition of their societal role, such as guerrilla warfare, can open new spaces and transform gender expectations in the post-movement society.

As will be more thoroughly explored in the next and final chapter, the transformation of gendered relations and roles has been a mixed-bag in the cases of South Africa and the United States. The high level of involvement of African women in the anti-apartheid, civil rights, and Black Power movements further undermined the legitimacy of a dichotomized understanding of gender. These efforts further entrenched activism as a part of the construction of African/Black Womanhood. The separation of the private and public spheres, already an unreality for most women of African descent, was further eroded by wielding the "private as political" through the strategic and militant use of motherhood, education, and consumer power. However, even with the successes of these movements in the areas of expanded political, economic, and social rights for African women and men, there have been regressive efforts to reassert patriarchies. While gender has become a more visible aspect of and strategy in the movements for racial equity and national liberation in the United States and South Africa, this visibility has been complicated and uneven.

CHAPTER 6

Repercussions: Gendered Interests and Social Movement Outcomes

The state may not unfairly discriminate directly or indirectly against anyone on one or more grounds, including race, gender sex, pregnancy, marital status, ethnic or social origin, colour, sexual orientation, age disability, religion, conscience, belief, culture language and birth. (The Constitution of the Republic of South Africa, 1996)

Viewing Gender in Social Movement Outcomes

The new South African constitution articulates the objectives toward which most anti-apartheid activists were struggling—a nonracial democracy. By the mid-1980s, the ruling Nationalist Party was forced to contend with mounting internal and external pressures. After centuries of White political rule, the 1994 election voted the African National Congress (ANC) in as the ruling political party in the South African Parliament and accelerated the process of restructuring South Africa into a nonracial, nonsexist, democratic republic. This political transformation has meant the end to explicitly racist social policies and repression against the non-White South African population and improved the political access and economic opportunities for African, Coloured, and Indian people in the country. It also opened a space for discussion and debate on a wide range of issues including "women's role within the negotiations and women's place in the new South Africa" (Meer 1998, 17). However, South Africa continues to be plagued by severe racial polarization, gender oppression, and class inequality. The negotiated settlement between the ANC and the ruling Nationalist

Party during the transfer of power left the majority of the land and economic resources in the hands of the same White business and agricultural elite while the majority of African people remain impoverished (Younis 2000). With respect to gender, at the same time that the new South African government boasts of one of the highest levels of representation of women in Parliament, it also has one of the highest rates of gender violence and poverty among women.

The outcomes of the civil rights and Black Power movements in the United States are equally complicated. On the one hand, the efforts on the part of African American activists and organizations for racial equality succeeded in eliminating the most flagrant and blatant forms of racial discrimination. On paper, the major objectives of the civil rights movement were met. Racial segregation, restrictions to voting and political participation, and discrimination in housing and employment were abolished by the courts and governmental decree. During the 1970s and early 1980s, the opening of educational and business opportunities resulted in the growth of an African American middle class and, for a period, reduced racial and gender gaps in wealth, income, and education (Bush 1998). In addition, the civil rights and Black Power movements stimulated the development of a number of spillover movements such as the women's, gay and lesbian, Chicano, and American Indian movements. At the same time, though, the more far-reaching types of social transformations envisioned by the more radical segment of the civil rights and Black Power movements were not achieved. As movement demands shifted from just eliminating racial barriers to economic and political redistribution, returns on demands diminished. This more militant phase of the racial liberation movement ended, not as a result of its mission being accomplished, but as a combined result of violent repression by the U.S. government's Counter Intelligence Program (COINTELPRO) and the co-optation of movement leaders, activists, and organizations. By the 1990s, the racial and gender gaps that had shown signs of narrowing a decade earlier in income and earnings, access to higher education, and employment began to reopen. The economic polarization that characterized the late 1980s and 1990s increased racial, ethnic, and gender competition and inequality. Reminiscent of an earlier era, new social movements have emerged to contend with remaining expressions of race, gender, and class inequality such as feminized and racialized poverty and the right-wing conservative backlash that has swept the country.

It is evident, then, that social movements vary in the degree of success that they achieve in accomplishing their desired objectives. Internally, the movement's organizational structure, composition, strategies, and political ideology play a role in determining the direction and extend of social change. On the other side, the external response to the movement on the part of the power structure and the perceptions and/or support of the larger public also has an impact. Gendered dynamics, both internal and external to the movement, further complicate social movement outcomes. The structural and ideational differences in the life experiences of women and men are intertwined with movement outcome factors in ways that preclude a simplistic determination of movement success or failure. Even if not directly focused on gender, social movement outcomes can be differentially experienced and perceived by women and men in the movement and/or the society. Perceptions about a movement or organization on the basis of the gender of its participants can impact its outcome in ways that either facilitate or hamper achievement of movement objectives. Finally, as movement participants are mobilized and engaged in social struggles, they transform and reconstruct gender relations, an outcome which may have been unintended. In some cases, the result is greater equality between women and men, while in other instances, gender inequalities and conservatism are strengthened.

This chapter explores the ways in which gendered relations and roles are implicated in social movement outcomes and effects. What are the gendered legacies and results of social movements? In what relative ways do women and men differentially benefit as a result of their participation in social resistance and/or the impact of this resistance on the wider society? Do social movements reflect, impact, or change gendered roles, relationships, and power dynamics? This final chapter addresses these questions keeping the concept of gendered interests in mind—that is, the relative stakes that factor into how movement outcomes and social transformations are experienced on both structural and subjective levels by women and men in a society. I conclude the chapter with observations on the view of social movements through a gender lens and commentary on the directions and trends that currently characterize gendered social movement research.

Gendered Interests: Strategic, Practical, and Interactive

Until recently, the outcomes of social movements were treated as if they were universally experienced both in the larger society and in the movement. Thus, very little attention was paid to the possibility of divergent and contradictory interests in the mix of outcomes that result from resistance struggles. Why would the outcomes of social movements differ for women and men? On some levels, they do not. There are basic social needs common to both women and men that are pursued by organized efforts to create social change: political rights, access to resources, and freedom from persecution. However, differences in the stakes that particular socially positioned groups (i.e., gender, race/ethnic, class, cultural) have in the types and levels of social change that the social movement engenders do differ. These respective "interests" have been described by Maxine Molyneux (1985) as "gender interests," that is, "those that women (or men) may develop by virtue of their social positioning through gender attributes" (Molyneux 1985, 283–4). The concept is based on the assumption that divisions of labor and separate spheres of social responsibility place differential importance on particular movement outcomes for women and men. In essence, gender standpoint and social positioning interacts with race, ethnicity, and class to differentially prioritize particular social needs.

In her exploration of the relative experience of women and men in the aftermath of socialist revolutions, Molyneux distinguished between two types of gender interests: "practical" and "strategic." "Practical" gender interests are associated with an immediate perceived need as related to gendered roles and responsibilities (Molyneux 1985). For instance, because of their responsibilities for the welfare of dependent children or because they hold specific positions in the labor market, women often have particularly high stakes in movement outcomes that affect these areas of life, for example. According to Molyneux,

> By virtue of their place within the sexual division of labor, women are disproportionately responsible for childcare and family health, and they are particularly concerned with housing and food provision. (Molyneux 1985, 298)

Just as women were more likely than men to be spurred into action in South Africa over the rising food prices in the 1940s and housing dislocations in the 1970s, they have been particularly interested in movement outcomes that addressed these issues. The practical gender interests in having shelter for the family underlay the actions the resident women of the Crossroads community took to resist the demolition during the 1970s and 1980s.

Similarly, in the United States, women of African descent were pursuing practical needs in their efforts to ride Montgomery, Alabama's, buses safely and with dignity. Later, in the post-civil rights/Black Power era, African Americans were active in the Welfare Rights movement which was mainly concerned with securing basic needs. The National Welfare Rights Organization (NWRO), formed in 1967, brought together impoverished African American women to deal with their practical gender and class interests. Local Welfare Rights Organizations sprouted up all over the country to deal with issues that were related to their economic, racial, and gender status that included substandard housing, harassment by social service staff, and job training needs.

In contrast, strategic gender interests are those that are vested in more fundamental and long-term transformations of gender hierarchies and inequities. These interests are linked to transforming the underlying bases of inequality that sustain the oppression of women and other disadvantaged groups: that is, maldistribution of resources (e.g., wealth/income, employment, and housing), uneven divisions of labor, and differential access to political power. Practical interests "do not in themselves challenge the prevailing forms of gender subordination, even though they arise directly out of them" while strategic gender interests do (Molyneux 1995, 284). The shift in power from the Nationalist Party to the African National Congress that occurred in 1994 South African elections, for example, promised to more fundamentally address gender inequities. To the degree that the new South African government changes the distribution of land, for example, it would address the strategic gender interests of women who were differentially affected by the South African policy of forced removals and the demolition of squatter's camps. In the case of the United States, the reformist outcomes of the movement have limited the social changes mostly to the level of practical gender interests.

The delineation of strategic versus practical gender interests can be a useful, but oversimplified, framework from which to assess social movement outcomes. Scholars have argued that this dichotomous view of interests fails to appreciate the complexity of the interaction between the immediate expressions and the structural grounding of gender inequality.

> The distinction between practical and strategic interests has been criticized by post-colonial feminists who argue that they tend to reproduce hierarchical dualisms that divide the personal from the political, the private from the public. (Peterson and Runyan 1999, 178)

Gendered interests are more continuous, dynamic, and interrelated than the "practical versus strategic" comparison describes. For women of African descent, the public/private split is itself problematic. For instance, the women's protests at the Crossroads squatter's camp in South Africa aimed at resisting immediate displacement from their residential community were geared primarily at the practical gender interest level; but the organizational structures that emerged—such as the Surplus People Project—continued to struggle for more substantial land redistribution and helped to frame the housing and land issues with which the government still wrestles.

This interaction between practical and strategic gender interests is evident in the Black Panther Party survival programs. Initiated in the late 1960s, these programs provided the community with services such as free breakfasts for youth, escort services for the elderly, health care and screening, and educational enrichment. Practical gender interests evidenced in these activities helped to perform some of the "expressive" and nurturing labor of the community that is associated with, and would have likely been performed by, women. These activities were also perceived by some in the party as associated with the "feminine," or soft side, of politics. JoNina Abron, BPP member and editor of the *Black Panther Intercommunal News Service*, has argued that "[s]ome members, including Eldridge Cleaver, favored an offensive military policy over the self-help activities of the survival programs" (Abron 1998, 179). However, as many Panther members and supporters have pointed out, these programs did not merely have survival in and of itself as a major objective, but as a means toward a greater and more far-reaching objective, that is, the total restructuring of the economic and political systems. In a word, revolution. As Huey Newton explained, "we called them survival programs pending revolution. . . . They were designed to help the people survive until their consciousness is raised, which is the first step in the revolution to produce a new America" (quoted in Abron 1998, 179). Presumably, this new society would be free of systematic inqualities on the basis of race, class, *and* gender.

The notion of "gendered interests" can be used as a matrix that is inclusive of strategic and practical interests interactively in order to describe the divergent stakes that women and men have in movement outcomes. In the analysis that follows, my emphasis will be placed on the interaction and continuum of gender interests, even when pointing out the strategic or practical implications of an outcome in relation to gendered relations, Conceiving of gender interests as comprehensive—that is, as strategic, practical, and interactive—helps us to assess the full range of ways in which social movement outcomes are gender differentiated.

Racial and National Liberation:
What's Gender Got to Do with It?

Social movement outcomes are gendered even when the movement is not primarily concerned with gender equality and women's liberation. Just as women and men have differential power and position within the movements to bring about change, they often share differentially in the rewards that result from movement efforts. With racial and national liberation movements, gender equality and/or women's empowerment is not an automatic outcome. Scholars and activists have asked, "To what extent have movements that obtained some degree of national independence or transformation in race/ethnic relations differentially benefited women and men?" (McFadden 1992; Molyneux 1985; Murray 1979). As Cynthia Enloe reminds us,

> Women do not benefit automatically every time the international system is re-ordered by a successful nationalist movement. It has taken awareness, questioning and organizing by women inside those nationalist movements to turn nationalism into something good for women. (Enloe 1989, 13)

During most liberation struggles, to the degree that gender equality or women's liberation is considered an outcome at all, it is viewed as contingent on the achievement of national sovereignty and independence. National liberation movements often express "gendered nationalism," or male domination in social movement structures becomes replicated in the post-movement processes and structures of the state apparatus (Gaidzanwa 1993; McFadden 1992; Peterson 1994). According to Ruth Meena, in post-colonial Southern African nations such as Zimbabwe and Mozambique,

> repression against women has been reinforced because of the weaknesses inherent in women's organizations during the post-colonial period. Most states in this region did not willingly create space for women's organizations to emerge as autonomous political organizations to fight for women's rights. Governments hijacked the women's movements by creating women's political wings of the ruling party as the only legitimate forum for women. (Meena 1992, 18)

After "independence," women and men often have different relationship to the state, the conceptualization of citizenship, and individual rights.

At the same time, a certain degree of gender equity or, at least, relaxation of gender restrictions, is often necessary to insure some measure of success in the struggle for national/racial independence. Sometimes for these purposes alone, national liberation struggles alter the relative social statuses of women and men in different and complex ways (Kuumba and Alston 1995).

The societies that emerge from racial and national liberation movements span a virtual continuum of gendered possibilities that can characterize social movement outcomes if we use women's progress as a gauge. Women's post-movement status takes different forms. For instance,

> Sometimes this alteration has consisted of a small step forward, as in Chile during the Allende years or in Mozambique after the victory against colonialism; sometimes it is a great leap forward, as in Cuba and China; and sometimes it is a step forward and then back again, as in Algeria. (Kuumba and Alston-Dosunmu 1995, 124)

The gendered outcome continuum can be described as: regression and/or repression optation; and/or progressive transformation.

A regressive gender outcome refers to the situation in which gender statuses and opportunities are equalized during the process of the social movement itself but, afterwards, the society returns to a high level of gender inequality and patriarchy is strengthened. In this case, the movement addresses neither practical nor strategic gender interests. Repression of women and increased gender inequality, often promoted in the name of "culture" and tradition, is used to undermine whatever transformations were made during the liberation struggle. National liberation, in cases such as these, leads to the downgrading of women's status and rekindled "traditional" patriarchal practices and structures (Rowbotham 1992; Gilliam 1991).

The Algerian revolution and its aftermath are used as the quintessential example of the regression and repression gendered outcome. In the case of Algeria, the cultural restrictions and social controls on Algerian women were relaxed in order to encourage their participation in the national liberation struggle. The post-movement status of women was much different.

> Most observers agree that the participation of women in the National Liberation Army (FLN) resulted primarily from the danger various missions posed to men. Women were recruited as the sisters, wives, and mothers of men who were members of the FLN, not as autonomous individuals in their own right. . . . At the advent of liberation, Algerian women continue to be treated as second-class citizens. The status of women in Algeria does not seem to be improving. In fact, Algerian women may, with respect to their sexual liberation, be worse off today than they were over two decades ago. (Kuumba and Alston-Dosunmu 1995, 113–4)

Although the regression does not dominantly describe the gendered movement outcomes in either the South African or U.S. cases, each society has experienced a sexist and misogynistic backlash at different points near the end or after their respective national/racial liberation movements. The "democratic transition" in South Africa, which brought record numbers of women into parliamentary and municipal government, for example, has been accompanied by heightened levels of violence against women. At the same time that a very progressive revised South African constitution forbids discrimination on the basis of race, gender, and sexual orientation, there has been an increase in sexual violence and anti-women practices such as "witch-burning." This practice has been increasingly used in rural areas to harass women who are viewed as powerful or independent. They are labeled as "witches" and often are attacked or have their houses set afire. There were backlashing efforts used in the latter part of the U.S. racial liberation movement to repress the Black feminist movement that developed in the 1970s and 1980s. The emergence of Black feminist structures like the Combahee collective, a group of Black feminists that was organized in 1974 in Boston, Massachusetts, was met with hostility by Black male scholars and activist leaders (Staples 1979).

To the degree that these changes improve conditions or distribute new advantages for some segment of the society, we can speak of "progress" (Gamson 1975). Movements for national liberation generally seek political and economic independence from a foreign colonizer. Under this broad objective, there are usually different experiences on the parts of women and men with respect to the ability to take advantage of these structural gains. The progress and transformation gendered outcome describes sustained advantage experienced by women in the aftermath of the movement. Structural societal changes that result from resistance activities can range from reforms such as enacting or repealing legislation to the full-scale transformation of the production and distribution of resources.

A number of factors both external and internal to the movement influence the degree to which movement outcomes ultimately address gender interests. The degree to which the movement structure and ideology allow for gender symmetry impacts the scope, form, and content of women's participation in the national liberation movement and the post-movement society (Kuumba and Alston 1995). In her analysis of Latin American resistance struggles, Lobao (1990) found that the mass participation in the Nicaraguan revolution, as opposed to the vanguard or limited scope of the movements in Cuba and Columbia, made a difference both in the involvement of women and in their post-movement society's commitment to gender interests. The Sandinista National Liberation Front (FSLN), which boasted of close to thirty percent female participation, created internal organizational space for women's participation in the form of the Association of Women Confronting the National Problem (AMPRONAC) and made the elimination of gender discrimination one of its long-term objectives (Lobao 1990).

The internal aspects of a movement operate within a larger social context and environment that has to be taken into account (Marx 1982). External to the movement, the political, economic, and cultural milieu of the society also impacts the way in which gendered interests are prioritized. The social environmental forces can inhibit or facilitate overall social movement success, as well as its ability to sustain gendered transformations. Countermovement forces can respond to movement efforts with everything from manipulation of the movement's public image and its access to resources and facilities, to outright sabotage and violence against participants (Marx 1982). The effects of these responses can be differentially applied and experienced by gender, in concert with other social divisions and relations—e.g., race, class, and nation.

These internal and external factors have to be taken into account in determining the extent to which gendered interests were addressed in the outcomes of the South African and United States national/racial liberation movements.

Civil Rights and Anti-Apartheid Outcomes

The civil rights/Black Power and anti-apartheid movements had the elimination of racial inequality and national oppression as their primary objectives. Neither of these movements completely achieved its objectives although, in both cases, progress has been made. The racial/national liberation movements in South Africa and the United States can both be considered "unfinished revolutions" to large degrees. They both resulted in "negotiated settlements" in which some reforms lessened the severity of racial domination but unequal distribution of wealth, resources, and power on the basis of race, ethnicity, and gender remain. In effect,

> the two liberation struggles are at a similar stage—significant progress has been made but major challenges still remain. . . . There are a number of similarities between post-Jim Crow black America and post-apartheid black South Africa. Legalized segregation has been abolished for all time, just as

racial slavery was in the previous century. The right of blacks to vote and hold office has been assured. But in both cases whites retain sufficient power to prevent either society from moving decisively and quickly beyond legal and political rights for all to the achievement of social and economic equality. (Fredrickson 1995, 320)

These movement outcomes have differed in the degree to which gender issues have been addressed and/or incorporated. The racial liberation movement in the United States has been much more stubborn in incorporating and addressing gendered interests than has the South African anti-apartheid movement and national reconstruction.

Gender Activism in the New South Africa: The Politics of Inclusion

From 1976 to 1989, the anti-apartheid movement went into "high gear," turned even more toward its community and township base, and took an increasingly diversified form. The resurgence of the trade union movement and emergence of numerous other organizations, including women's organizations and community-level and grassroots programs, led to a renewed cycle of protest. Specifically, the Black Consciousness Movement-inspired Soweto uprising of 1976, and the governmental reaction to it, ushered in a new movement phase. On June 16, students in this township near Johannesburg held a peaceful protest against being educated in Afrikaans, the language of the Dutch-descended "Boers." Government security forces responded to the protest harshly by shooting, wounding, and killing many unarmed youth; subsequently, related movement organizations and individuals were banned. Movement response was quite different this time:

> Unlike what happened after Sharpeville, the repression that followed Soweto did not lead to a long period of political inactivity and apparent black resignation in the face of overwhelming white power. Soweto in fact is now recognized as a turning point in recent South African history. (Fredrickson 1995, 309)

After the 1976 Soweto uprising, "the character of the mass struggle in South Africa . . . developed dramatically. It [was] a decade in which workers, youth, and women have distinguished themselves by their militancy" (Kimble and Unterhalter 1982, 30). A cross-generational, gender-inclusive, and broader movement character emerged that was characterized by an upsurge of movement activity and increased unity among the various movement sectors (Frederickson 1995; Kimble and Unterhalter 1982; Taylor 1997).

The heightened level of the struggle widened the range of resistance activities engaged in by women in gender-integrated and parallel organizations. For instance, the Federation of South African Women (FSAW) was reconstituted on the Western Cape region in 1985 and focused its attention on violence against women and women political prisoners (Fester 1997). Resistance against forced removals staged by women of the Crossroads Committee at Crossroads squatter's camp outside the city of Capetown in 1978, in which women blocked bulldozers from destroying their houses, illustrates a different site in the range of community resistance that arose. In this context of mass struggle, women and their organizations were absorbed and embraced within the larger nationalist project. A scholar at the University of Witwatersrand explains,

> During the 1980s, women played a very prominent role in organizations and in the struggles against repression. Women had by that time been considerably influenced by the experiences of women's organizations and the women's movements in many parts of the world. This had sparked a debate about the necessity of organizing as women. (Meintjes 1998, 74)

Expanded sites for movement participation provided the milieu for the incorporation of gender equality as a major priority in the democratic transition that characterized the post-apartheid movement phase.

The cycle of protest that dynamically linked internal activism with external and international pressure culminated in the period of negotiation that began in the late 1980s and early 1990s. Unity between the various civic movements, student groups, community organizations, trade unions, and cultural/sports clubs became official with the establishment of the United Democratic Front (UDF) in 1983. In the early 1980s, under the umbrella of the UDF, organizations and informal networks of African people engaged in a "people's war" in which "people in their own sectors of activity could contribute by resisting within their own areas" (Jeffery 1991). The range of strategies used during this period was vast including demonstrations, strikes, stayaways, rent and other economic boycotts, and school disruptions. The Congress of South African Trade Unions (COSATU), a major force within the UDF, was joined by church groups, youth and student organizations, street committees, and cultural organizations. The overall strategy of mass action was to make apartheid ungovernable, leading ultimately toward social transformation. The UDF accelerated the pace of movement so much that, by the end of the decade, the South African government was forced to negotiate with the liberation forces. After the liberation movement organizations were unbanned on February 11, 1990, the fervor of the movement escalated and the range of strategic opportunities increased (Taylor 1997). By August of that same year, the ANC Women's League had been relaunched. What followed was a proliferation of local, nongovernmental, and governmental structures that addressed gender or women's issues in some way. Each of these organizations addresses a particular aspect of women's lives such as poverty, domestic abuse, and health care.

The 1990 Malibongwe Conference in Amsterdam which took place during this transitional phase was organized to insure that women's issues were included in the political transition to democracy and power sharing. This was the phasing in of a different political climate which entailed a transition from mobilizing women for the national struggle to actually addressing gender issues within national policy and reconstruction. As part of this process, the Women's National Coalition (WNC) was formed in 1992 as an umbrella for a broad spectrum of women's organizations. This multiracial entity served as a gender watchdog during the period of constitutional negotiations. Between 1992 and 1994, the WNC engaged in a participatory research project in which focus groups were held around the country to gather information from South African women of varied backgrounds about the issues that were most pressing in their lives (Women's National Coalition 1994). The WNC found that women were concerned with poverty and the cost of living, employment opportunities, racial and class differences in housing and standards of living, and subordination and violence in partnerships. They were particularly concerned with the customary laws that defined women as perpetual minors and limited their ability to inherit property, enter into contracts, or seek divorce. Gaidzanwa (1993, 56) explains that, in southern Africa, "access to nationality and citizenship has been predicated on race, class, and gender." By colonial and traditional law, African women were forbidden in many instances from political, land ownership, and child custody rights. In South Africa, the practice of *lobola*, the custom of economic exchange on the part of a man for his wife, is an example. Women surveyed in 1992 by the Women's National Coalition felt that the practice should be abolished since it leads men to treat women as if they have been purchased (Women's National Coalition 1994). Through this mechanism, women's organizations and wings of movement organizations were able to voice their perspectives and continually infuse the principle of gender equality as integral to the concept of a "new South Africa" (Kemp et al. 1995; Taylor 1997). The Government of National Unity led by the ANC which took power in May 1994 had to not only contend with but address this high level of gender activism. In response, the ANC established the Commission on Gender Equity (CGE) to educate and agitate on issues contributing toward gender equality and concerning women. During its first few years of existence, this organizational body embarked on a "Programme of Action" which targeted the most disadvantaged women in the society—African women in the rural areas. Although inequities and hardships remain, the CGE cited the 1998 passing of the Customary Marriages, Domestic Violence and Maintenance Acts, which protected women from abuse and granted them rights to inheritance in traditional unions, as a major victory from their work. Learning from other newly independent nations' mistakes, the new South African government has opted to establish a "gender desk" in every department in hopes that this will lessen the tendency to marginalize gender issues, which occurs when separate women's ministries are created within the governmental structure (Meintjes 1998).

The "democratic transition" that had extended South African citizenship in racialized and gendered ways is a direct and observable outcome of the anti-apartheid movement. Since 1994, the ANC-led government commitment to forging a nonracial democracy has been accompanied by efforts to close the gender gaps, as well. This transition in the struggle from resistance to negotiation opened up additional space for gendered activism (Kemp et al. 1995; Meintjes 1998).

> What emerged from this period of reassessment and re-positioning, and as a great surprise to many, was the proliferation of women's organizations and a strong call for a more coherent women's movement to push gender issues onto the nation's agenda for transformation. . . . these "opportunities" and "spaces" were themselves a result of hard struggle around gender issues in the period leading up to the Conference of a Democratic South Africa (CODESA) talks. (Primo 1997, 32)

An additional structural outcome of social movement activity has been the growth of gender-focused organizations and movement structures accompanied by a transformation with existing organizations (Tarrow 1995).

The recent shifts in South African power relations have opened new spaces for the articulation of gender issues (Kemp et al. 1995). As a result, there has been a proliferation of gender and women's organizations in the post-apartheid era. The Women's National Coalition (WNC), Commission on Gender Equality (CGE), Rural Women's Movement (RWM), and United Women's Congress are but a few of these emergent entities. These structural outcomes of the national liberation movement increase the potential of gender issues serving as a priority for the post-apartheid government.

The Women's National Coalition, an umbrella for a wide spectrum of women's organizations, was created to mitigate against women's exclusion from the negotiation process. Its "charter campaign" of 1992 was developed to

> acquire and disseminate information about women's needs and aspirations, and secondly, to unify women in formulating and adopting a charter or other document and entrench effective equality in the construction of South Africa. (WNC 1994, 20)

The resulting blueprint for achieving transformational gendered outcomes and post-apartheid gender equity, the Women's Charter for Effective Equality, was adopted by the WNC in February 1994. According to South African scholar Sheila Meintjes, the Charter helped to shape the new South African constitution and "redefined the notion of equality in terms of women's differentiated needs" (Meintjes 1998, 81). Later, the Commission on Gender Equality (CGE), established in 1997 as mandated in the new South African constitution, was given the task of promoting and developing gender equality. While not a panacea for eliminating the combined inequalities of gender and race, the development of this and other organizations with the distinct objectives of infusing the new government and constitution with concern for women's lives illustrates a gender consciousness that developed through the struggles over gender hierarchies and power differentials during the process of the movement.

In addition to the development of new organizations and networks, there has been gendered transformation within existing structures, as well. Trade Unions such as the South African Commercial, Catering and Allied Workers' Union (SACCAWU), a union of African workers in the retail and catering industry organized by Emma Mashinini in 1975, has been in the forefront of the struggle for gender equity. They have implemented programs to close the gender gap in leadership, conscientize its members about the realities of sexism in the workplace, and pressure employers to adopt gender-friendly policies such as family leave and child care. As early as 1989, SACCAWU passed a "Resolution on the Oppression of Women" which challenged both women and men to promote gender equality within the union. In 1997, SACCAWU began a three-year gender empowerment training program which included workshops on the basics of gender, economic literacy, and collective bargaining geared toward increasing the proportion of women in union leadership.

The current political changes, when placed within the context of South Africa's tainted history, are indeed impressive. In addition to an African-led government, South Africa has gone "from being one of the world's most sexist governments [to one in which] our new Parliament, with its 106-strong contingent of women, has emerged as one of the world's most progressive" (Kemp et al. 1995, 154). In the most recent period, South Africa can be described as highly gender conscious. Only time will tell the degree to which this consciousness becomes manifest in action and real transformation of the gross inequalities by gender, race, and class that continue to plague the society. The outcome in the case of South Africa has been an explicit inclusion of gender equity as a platform of the African National Congress since their ascendance to power. According to Charman, De Swardt, and Simons in their analysis of the 1990 Malibongwe Conference papers, "The ANC in its understanding of the political importance of women is more advanced than any other political organisation in South Africa" (Charman, De Swardt, and Simons 1991, 2).

Black Feminism as Movement Outcome

The racial liberation struggle in the United States took a different direction with respect to gender consciousness and women's liberation as outcome. An embryonic Black women's/feminist movement was initiated as early as 1968 with the establishment of the Black Women's Liberation Committee, which was followed by the emergence of the Third World Women's Alliance in 1969, organized by former women of SNCC, the National Feminist Organization in 1973, and the Combahee River Collective in 1974 (Evans 1979; Giddings 1984; Roth 1999; Springer 2001). These rumblings surfaced more fully in the phase from 1975 to 1995, which saw a general decline in the race/class liberation sector of the movement and an upsurge of racialized gender consciousness. By the mid-1970s, the broader racial/nationalist movement had reached a low ebb. Through the Federal Bureau of Investigation's (FBI) Counter Intelligence Program (COINTELPRO), police harassment and attacks combined with infiltration to destabilize the movement (Seale 1968). The embryonic gender consciousness of 1964 emerged as a full-scale women's liberation movement from the embers of the racial liberation struggle. This gender split itself split racially. Brewer has identified this phenomenon as "the historic path of Black feminist development in the second wave of U.S. feminism" (Brewer 1993, 15). Formed in the early 1970s, the Combahee River Collective and National Black Feminist Organization viewed themselves as philosophically different from such so-called mainstream White feminist organizations as the National Organization for Women (NOW) (hooks 1981, 1984). As a result of a history of struggle against multiple oppressions, the Black feminist formations proposed a need for developing a new movement with an understanding of the complexities of multiplicative racial/ethnicity, class, sexuality, and gender dynamics.

Throughout the 1980s and early 1990s, the development of a critical Black feminist discourse, incubated in these autonomous African American women's collectives, took "center stage" in the movement. On the other side of the gender split in the movement during this era was a separatist masculinized politics of cultural nationalism, which reasserted the patriarchy and conservative nationalism as the movement's objective. This period, particularly the early 1980s, was also characterized by a rise in movement activity and a broadened internationalist and Pan-African consciousness in the African diaspora. The rise of the anti-apartheid solidarity activity and an increase in Afrocentric and African nationalist/liberationist organizations on college campuses and in communities repopularized liberation and oppositional ideologies, identity movements, and their associated aesthetics and symbols. At the same time, the movement deconstructed into various fragmented segments—revolutionary pan-Africanism, cultural nationalism, Black feminism, Black Marxists, Black Gays and Lesbians.

We can identify 1995 as a transition point in the U.S. national/racial liberation movement. This most current phase of the movement began with the Million Man March which took place in Washington, D.C., in 1995, as a "Holy Day of Atonement and Reconciliation." While the Million Man March served as a strong symbol of continued dissatisfaction with U.S. race relations and included selected African American women as participants and organizers, it flowed from the conservative and patriarchal traditions in the movement (Lusane 1997). The stated objective of having African American men atone for their transgressions and assume family and community responsibilities was based on an underlying assumption of individual-level causation for the plight of African Americans. While the gender segregationist tone was softened as the time of the march approached, the original call which excluded African American women was hotly contested in the Black community.

> Although women did much of the work of organizing the march—as has been the case historically in black politics—the march explicitly privileged the plight of the most serious issue facing African Americans, and women were asked to stay at home that day and educate the children. . . . The problem, in a larger sense, was the political exclusion of black women's issues and concerns. . . . The politics of the march's leaders essentially said that only issues facing black men were issues for the whole black community, while the issues facing black women were not. (Lusane 1997, 205)

This position is reminiscent of an earlier phase in the movement which, essentially, premised the liberation of African American people on the rejuvenation of the Black patriarchy and male dominance.

In part, the Million Women's March (MWM), held in Philadelphia in 1997, was a response to the exclusionary gender politics of the MMM (Campbell 1997). While directed toward African American women, the focus of this march was around general community issues rather than on "gender" or women's oppression *per se*. Both the Million Man and the Million Women's Marches played on gender-separated racial politics in their agendas for pursuing social justice.

At the same time, learning from the errors of the past, there are growing tendencies in the movement toward a progressive gender-conscious politics.

> Women's wings and organizations such as the All-African Women's Revolutionary Union (AAWRU or the "Union"), the U.S. based women's wing of the All-African People's Revolutionary Party (AAPRP) established in 1980, emerged specifically to address this question of women's oppression and liberation in the Pan-African movement. Its emergence was reflective of the tension within the Pan-African movement between African nationalism, women's liberation, and class struggle. While the formation of the AAWRU represented a qualitative leap in gendering Pan-Africanism, it also heightened old struggles around African women's roles in the movement thus creating new gender/race/class contradictions. (Kuumba 1999)

As another example, in 1998 close to 2,000 activists of African descent attended the Black Radical Congress (BRC) held in Chicago under the thematic banner, "Setting a Black Radical Agenda for the 21st Century." The BRC is a contemporary attempt to "reinvigorate and redirect the movement toward liberation" (Cha-Jua 1998, 9). An important transformation that the BRC represents in the movement is an inclusive appreciation for some of the very lines which split the earlier phases of the NLM in the United States, like gender. An attending activist reported, for example, that

> [g]ender, especially the concerns of women are central to the BRC's theory, strategy, and tactics. The Black Radical Congress is being structured on gender equality. Most roles or functional positions in the BRC consist of women and men co-chairs. (Cha-Jua 1998, 10)

The Black Radical Congress is the first national level, gender-integrated coalition of African American activists and organizations to put "anti-sexism" and the eradicating of women's oppression in the forefront of its mission (Hamer and Neville 1998, 22). On the structural level, not only was women's representation at leadership levels a priority, a Black Feminist Caucus was created to spearhead the refining of Black Revolutionary Feminism. In the United States, women's wings and organizations such as the All-African Women's Revolutionary Union (AAWRU, or the "Union"), the U.S.-based women's wing of the All-African People's Revolutionary Party (AAPRP, established in 1980), and the Black Feminist Caucus of the Black Radical Congress (1998) represent an imploding of these contradictions. These parallel women-only structures emerged within gender-integrated liberation organizations to specifically address this question of women's oppression. Their emergence is reflective of the tensions within the Black Liberation Movement among nationalism, women's liberation, and class struggle.

Gender Divergence in Outcomes: A Comparative Perspective

While the anti-apartheid and civil rights/Black Power movements were both concerned with transforming systems of racial/ethnic inequality, their outcomes also had implication for gendered interests, both structurally and ideologically. In both of these examples, the gendered nature of the broader political opportunity structure interacted with movement processes to catalyze the development of gender-separate and autonomous structures and a "gendering of consciousness." These movements differed radically, though, in the degree to which these gendered structures and consciousness interfaced with the broader national/racial liberation movement. In the South African case, the momentum of women's collective forms of activism was absorbed into the broad-based unity, and gender equality became a priority of the national reconstruction. In the post-civil rights/Black Power era, the U.S. racial justice movement has been more resistant to addressing gender oppression, in concert with racism and economic inequality.

Autonomous women's organizations and gendered consciousness developed as an outcome of the national/racial liberation movements in South Africa and the United States. The gendered hierarchies, power differentials, and divisions of labor in the society and movement had two structural outcomes: "explosion" into autonomous women's organs, and "implosion," resulting in the formation of women's wings, secretariats, and ministries internal to the gender-integrated organizations and political parties. In fact, nationalist movements are notorious for stimulating gendered consciousness and offshoot movements of autonomous or semi-autonomous women's movements and organizations (Evans 1979; Gilliam 1991; Jacquette 1994; Jayawardena 1986; Steady 1993). The postcolonial women's liberation movements and gender-focused nongovernmental organizations (NGOs) that proliferated in Africa, the African diaspora, Latin America, and the Caribbean in the post-colonial period were incubated in the context of national liberation struggles. While viewed as secondary to national liberation, official male-led movement organizations such as the African National Congress and the Student Nonviolent Coordinating Committee developed women's wings to specifically mobilize women and address their particular issues.

Many scholars who have studied women or gender in social movements have noted the dynamic of "gendering consciousness" as a movement outcome. The unfolding of gender struggles and women's political concerns and issues within racial/national liberation movements takes different paths on the basis of class location, culture, and historical period (Noonan 1995; Schirmer 1993). Thus frame transformation, or changes in the shared belief system, is a consequence and outcome of movement.

While this process can be understood on the level of individual consciousness, it can also be used to characterize the entire movement. In this latter case, it refers to an appreciation for the women's issues and the incorporation of women's liberation and gender equality into the movement's political consciousness and objectives. As women experience discrimination, limitations, or differential treatment in society and in male-dominated movement organizations, they become more aware of the effects of sexism and patriarchy. As has been observed, a gendered consciousness emerged as a force in the anti-apartheid movement in South Africa and in the civil rights and Black Power eras of U.S. struggle. The differences in the relationship between the gender consciousness and the racial/national liberation movements in the United States and South Africa, respectively, created divergent outcomes with respect to gender interests.

In both the South African anti-apartheid and the U.S. racial liberation movements, these gender-separate and integrated bodies forced the official structures and larger movements into action and more radical positions. During the latter phases of the anti-apartheid struggle, though, the emergence of community-based organizations and networks that were either predominantly women or that focused on women's issues and gender were included under the umbrella of the mass anti-apartheid struggle. With the background of the history of the pass-law demonstrations of the 1950s, the significance of women's contribution to the liberation movement was already part of the framing and collective understanding of the movement. From this basis, women's empowerment and gender equality were fused with the objectives of racial and class equality as a major priority of the new South African government. Addressing gender gaps became a project of all the major societal institutions: political parties, unions, educational institutions. A practical example of this is the work that the South African labor unions are currently doing to fuse gender into their efforts for worker's rights. Along with including the particular concerns of women workers, the International Labour Resource and Information Group (ILRIG) published "Weaving Gender into Our Work: A Handbook for Working People and Their Organizations" in 1996 to assist activists in integrating a gender perspective. According to the manual,

> Having a gender perspective is vital for the labour movement today. Women make up close to 40% of the world's workers in the formal economy. And in almost all countries, if we include housework, women work longer hours than men. Developments in world capitalism today, particularly in paid work, have had a significant effect on women. . . . These developments have also changed the nature and composition of the world's workers. Trade unions will have to respond to these changes and challenges. But they can only respond effectively if they integrate a gender perspective to their analysis and strategies. (MacQuene 1996, 1)

In the U.S. case, the distance between "racial" and "gender" issues remained in the post-civil rights/Black Power era. Very few of the major movement organizations, either in political platform or organizational structure, specifically linked gender issues to their nationalistic or social-istic objectives. As a result, the outcomes of the racial justice struggle in the U.S. case has been, and remains, much more divisive with respect to gender and women's liberation.

On the subjective level, in the U.S. black liberation movement, the gender awareness and consciousness that was heightened during the course of the movement activities was initially very racialized and was later marginalized (Evans 1979; Robnett 1998). For the most part, the Black feminist and White women's liberation movement developed as distinct and separate tracks out of the civil rights and Black Power movements (Roth 2000). Working and middle-class women of African descent, for whom issues of race and class remained salient, continued to participate in gender-integrated movements, even while participating also in autonomous, parallel women's organizations. As a result, the vibrant and dynamic race/class/gender analysis that emerged from this Black feminist discourse has yet to be fully integrated into the political project of racial liberation or women's movements as they are currently defined.

The racial/national liberation struggles in the United States and South Africa are clearly unfinished and uneven. What is evident from these examples is that their unevenness is not only evident in the degree to which national/racial liberation has been achieved, but also the degree to which gender interests—particularly those of a strategic nature—have been consciously linked to the movement. Unlike the South African reality, the gender split that emerged in the racial liberation movement in the United States during the mid-1960s into the early 1970s has never been fully mended. Women's empowerment and gender equality have yet to be viewed as central to the project of racial equality in the United States, as has become the case in South Africa. In many ways, the systems of oppression, which have been so clearly linked in the Black feminist discourse and many academic circles, has yet to make itself to the "streets" (Smith 2000).

Trends in Gendered Social Movement Research

Gendered analyses of social movements have generated critiques and viewpoints that continue to transform our understanding of the dynamics of social insurgence and transformation. As masculinist notions of social activism have been dismantled, strategies of social resistance and struggle that had previously been ignored have become more visible. Analyses that appreciate the gendered nature of political opportunities have added whole

new layers to our thinking of the conditions that spark movement participation. Theoretical frameworks that rethink the simplistic dichotomies
between leaders and followers have allowed for more textured analysis of
movement processes and the variable roles that women, in particular, have
played within them. Through a gender lens, the stories of movement leaders such as Ella Baker and Frances Baard, with whom we began this
discussion, become more central to the story. As we move into a new historical phase of activism, though, how will these lines of thinking be
extended? What directions will gendered social movement research and
action take in the years to come?

One of the most exciting trends in the development of gendered social
movement research is the placement of gender struggles and women's activism within the context of the globalized system. The globalization
process that has allowed transnational corporations to move freely across
borders for cheap labor has increased the level of poverty and inequality
in much of the world. Neither social policy nor social activism is currently
confined to the nation-state level. Sonia E. Alvarez's observation about Latin
American feminists illustrates this trend. According to her study,

> the 1990s witnessed the ascendance of a new form of international activism
> among growing numbers of feminists in the region—one targeting intergov-
> ernmental organizations (IGOs) and international policy arenas and thereby
> hoping to gain global leverage in pressuring for changes in gender policy
> on the home front. (Alvarez 2000, 29)

Researchers and activists have, as a result, become more interested in
transnational and regional women's organizations and their impact on global policy as well as on local conditions (Alvarez 2000; Basu 2000). Not only
are the structures and networks that characterize the transnational women's
movement of interest in this emerging area of study, but also the impact of
global exchange of ideas and culture on social mobilization.

At the same time that these global connections around issues of gender have been explored, social movement scholars have also been intrigued
by the gendered "local" and indigenous expressions of activism. Contemporary researchers are attempting to traverse the fine line between
universalist or sweeping generalizations and focus on the particularities
of specific social and historical contexts. There is a growing concern with
the diversity of mobilizations of women or concerning gender issues on
the "grassroots" level and the differing ways they address common "global" problems (Sinha et al. 1999). Studies that have documented

community-level mobilizations (Naples 1998a, 1998b) and activism from the standpoint of particular identities (Springer 1999) have been increasingly conscious of the problematic nature of overgeneralizations and the need to take historical, social, economic, and political context into account.

There are also trends in the scholarship to create a "systematic theory of gender and social movements" in order to better understand and appreciate: (1) the creation of gender hierarchies in organizational practices; (2) the role of gender stratification in the emergence of social movements; (3) collective identities within which gender is fused; and (4) the processes of resistance and challenge to oppressive gender relations (Taylor 1999). The ultimate objective of frameworks that can be used to understand the ways in which gender dynamics, in concert with those of race/ethnicity/class/culture, impede and catalyze insurgency goes beyond being an academic exercise. The incorporation of a dialectical analysis of gender in contemporary resistance struggles, when underpinned by a social justice commitment, can be a contributing force for social change and transformation.

Appendix 1

Women's Charter

Adopted at the Founding Conference of the Federation of
South African Women
Johannesburg, 17 April 1954[1]

Preamble: We, the women of South Africa, wives and mothers, working women and housewives, African, Indians, European and Coloured, hereby declare our aim of striving for the removal of all laws, regulations, conventions and customs that discriminate against us as women, and that deprive us in any way of our inherent right to the advantages, responsibilities and opportunities that society offers to any one section of the population.

A Single Society: We women do not form a society separate from the men. There is only one society, and it is made up of both women and men. As women we share the problems and anxieties of our men, and join hands with them to remove social evils and obstacles to progress.

Test of Civilisation: The level of civilisation which any society has reached can be measured by the degree of freedom that its members enjoy. The status of women is a test of civilisation. Measured by that standard, South Africa must be considered low in the scale of civilised nations.

Women's Lot: We women share with our menfolk the cares and anxieties imposed by poverty and its evils. As wives and mothers, it falls upon us to make small wages stretch a long way. It is we who feel the cries of our children when they are hungry and sick. It is our lot to keep and care for

---

[1] The Charter expressed the philosophy and aims of the newly established Federation of South African Women (FSAW). It was adopted at the inaugural conference and included in the final report of the conference.

141

the homes that are too small, broken and dirty to be kept clean. We know the burden of looking after children and land when our husbands are away in the mines, on the farms, and in the towns earning our daily bread.

We know what it is to keep family life going in pondokkies and shanties, or in overcrowded one-room apartments. We know the bitterness of children taken to lawless ways, of daughters becoming unmarried mothers whilst still at school, of boys and girls growing up without education, training or jobs at a living wage.

Poor and Rich: These are evils that need not exist. They exist because the society in which we live is divided into poor and rich, into non-European and European. They exist because there are privileges for the few, discrimination and harsh treatment for the many. We women have stood and will stand shoulder to shoulder with our menfolk in a common struggle against poverty, race and class discrimination, and the evils of the colour-bar.

National Liberation: As members of the National Liberatory movements and Trade Unions, in and through our various organisations, we march forward with our men in the struggle for liberation and the defence of the working people. We pledge ourselves to keep high the banner of equality, fraternity and liberty. As women there rests upon us also the burden of removing from our society all the social differences developed in past times between men and women, which have the effect of keeping our sex in a position of inferiority and subordination.

Equality for Women: We resolve to struggle for the removal of laws and customs that deny African women the right to own, inherit or alienate property. We resolve to work for a change in the laws of marriage such as are found amongst our African, Malay and Indian people, which have the effect of placing wives in the position of legal subjection to husbands, and giving husbands the power to dispose of wives' property and earnings, and dictate to them in all matters affecting them and their children.

We recognise that the women are treated as minors by these marriage and property laws because of ancient and revered traditions and customs which had their origin in the antiquity of the people and no doubt served purposes of great value in bygone times.

There was a time in the African society when every woman reaching marriageable stage was assured of a husband, home, land and security.

Then husbands and wives with their children belonged to families and clans that supplied most of their own material needs and were largely self-sufficient. Men and women were partners in a compact and closely-integrated family unit.

Women Who Labour: Those conditions have gone. The tribal and kinship society to which they belonged has been destroyed as a result of the loss of tribal land, migration of men away from their tribal home, the growth of towns and industries and the rise of a great body of wage-earners on the farms and in the urban areas, who depend wholly or mainly on wages for a livelihood.

Thousands of African women, like Indians, Coloured and European women, are employed today in factories, homes, offices, shops, on farms, in professions as nurses, teachers and the like. As unmarried women, widows or divorcees they have to fend for themselves, often without the assistance of a male relative. Many of them are responsible not only for their own livelihood but also that of their children.

Large numbers of women today are in fact the sole breadwinners and heads of their families.

Forever Minors: Nevertheless, the laws and practices derived from an earlier and different state of society are still applied to them. They are responsible for their own person and their children. Yet the law seeks to enforce upon them the status of a minor.

Not only are African, Coloured and Indian women denied political rights, but they are also in many parts of the Union denied the same status as men in such matters as the right to enter into contracts, to own and dispose of property, and to exercise guardianship over their children.

Obstacle to Progress: The law has lagged behind the development of society; it no longer corresponds to the actual social and economic position of women. The law has become an obstacle to progress of the women, and therefore a brake on the whole of society.

This intolerable condition would not be allowed to continue were it not for the refusal of a large section of our menfolk to concede to us women the rights and privileges which they demand for themselves.

We shall teach the men that they cannot hope to liberate themselves from the evils of discrimination and prejudice as long as they fail to extend to women complete and unqualified equality in law and in practice.

Need for Education: We also recognise that large numbers of our womenfolk continue to be bound by traditional practices and conventions, and fail to realise that these have become obsolete and a brake on progress. It is our duty and privilege to enlist all women in our struggle for emancipation and to bring to them all realisation of the intimate relationship that exists between their status of inferiority as women and the inferior status to which their people are subjected by discriminatory laws and colour prejudices.

It is our intention to carry out a nation-wide programme of education that will bring home to the men and women of all national groups the realisation that freedom cannot be won for any one section or for the people as a whole as long as we women are kept in bondage.

An Appeal: We women appeal to all progressive organisations, to members of the great National Liberatory movements, to the trade unions and working class organisations, to the churches, educational and welfare organisations, to all progressive men and women who have the interests of the people at heart, to join with us in this great and noble endeavour.

Our Aims

We declare the following aims:

This organisation is formed for the purpose of uniting women in common action for the removal of all political, legal, economic and social disabilities. We shall strive for women to obtain:

1. The right to vote and to be elected to all State bodies, without restriction or discrimination.
2. The right to full opportunities for employment with equal pay and possibilities of promotion in all spheres of work.
3. Equal rights with men in relation to property, marriage and children, and for the removal of all laws and customs that deny women such equal rights.
4. For the development of every child through free compulsory education for all; for the protection of mother and child through maternity homes, welfare clinics, creches and nursery schools, in countryside and towns; through proper homes for all, and through the provision of water, light, transport, sanitation, and other amenities of modern civilisation.
5. For the removal of all laws that restrict free movement, that prevent or hinder the right of free association and activity in democratic organisations, and the right to participate in the work of these organisations.

6. To build and strengthen women's sections in the National Liberatory movements, the organisation of women in trade unions, and through the peoples' varied organisation.

7. To cooperate with all other organisations that have similar aims in South Africa as well as throughout the world.

8. To strive for permanent peace throughout the world.

Appendix 2a

WHAT IS THE FIRST THING A MOTHER THINKS OF?

The answer is simple—a mother's first concern is for her child or unborn children.

She wants her children to have good food, proper clothes, a pleasant home; to be educated; to have opportunities for happiness and development.

No mother will rest content until she has won these things for her children.

HOW CAN WE GET WHAT WE WANT FOR OUR CHILDREN?

The time when women sat at home and wept or wished for better things for their children has long since passed.

Women are now in the forefront of the fight in our country for a better life for all, particularly for our children.

Large numbers of women worked day and night to make the great Congress of the People a success. More women than ever before were among the delegates from all over our country attending that Congress.

No people can win freedom while the women are kept back. No people can win happiness while the women are prevented from playing their part.

Our children's future depends on the extent to which we, the mothers of South Africa, organise and work and fight for a better life for our little ones.

WHAT MUST WE DO?

Recently, a World Congress of Mothers was held in Europe. Women from every country met to find ways to end wars, to build a peaceful and happy world. We South African women will meet to add our voices to those of other women in the world, so that we can express our opinions and seek solutions to the problems of our country and of mothers everywhere.

THE CONGRESS OF MOTHERS

On August 7th, Transvaal Mothers will meet. This is what they will discuss:

- What women can do to help carry out the Freedom Charter adopted at the Congress of the People.

- How we can campaign particularly for those sections of the Charter that call for "Houses, Security and Comfort!" and "The Doors of Learning and Culture shall be Opened!"
- How women of South Africa can help to preserve peace, to prevent the fearful and useless destruction of human life in war.
- How we women can strengthen and build our organisations and win recognition of our right to equal treatment and rights as human beings; how we can do away with laws and customs that keep women as inferiors.

WHO WILL BE THERE?

We call on every mother, every woman, to come to the Congress of Mothers. No woman will be debarred from attending. Every woman who has the future of her children, of the children of South Africa, at heart, is invited to attend this meeting.

SHOW THIS LEAFLET to women you know. Urge them to come. And see that you come yourself, on:

SUNDAY 7TH AUGUST, 9:30 A.M.
TRADES HALL NO. 3 (1st Floor), Kerk Street,
JOHANNESBURG.

IMPORTANT: PLEASE NOTE: Tea will be served at 3d cup, but you are asked to bring your own lunch—WE CANNOT SERVE LUNCHES. Bring sandwiches or other food for midday.

Federation of South African Women (Transvaal Region) P.O. Box 10876, Johannesburg.

WOMEN DON'T WANT PASSES!

Plans for the issue of passes to African women are now complete. WHEN YOU CARRY A PASS.....you may not move freely form place to place; you can be arrested at any time, day or night, for failing to produce your pass on demand; you become a SLAVE to police and government, who can order you to go where they please, to work where they demand. PASS LAWS DE-STROY FAMILY LIFE.

IN THE PAST, AFRICAN WOMEN HAVE ALWAYS SUCCESSFULLY RE-SISTED ATTEMPTS TO MAKE THEM CARRY PASSES. WE WILL NOT NOW BECOME SLAVES TO THE PASS LAWS!

Women of the Transvaal are going to Pretoria on THURSDAY 27th OC-TOBER, 1955, to put their demands to the Government. As WOMEN AND MOTHERS we are going to demand freedom of movement, the right to protest against pass laws, Bantu Education, and other unjust laws. We are going to demand the right to justice and happiness for every child in this country.

You are invited to join this mass protest of women of all races. Let the voice of women be heard clearly and loudly throughout the land, so that our legitimate demands are answered with justice!

If you have not already given your name in, fill in this form and hand it to your Branch Secretary of the African National Congress Women's League, post it direct to: P.O. BOX 10876, JOHANNESBURG.

I want to join the Women's Protest. Please send me more information.

NAME_____

ADDRESS_____

THE VOICE OF WOMEN WILL BE HEARD THROUGHOUT SOUTH AFRICA ON THE 27TH!

Appendix 2b

THE DEMAND OF THE WOMEN OF SOUTH AFRICA FOR THE WITHDRAWAL OF PASSES FOR WOMEN AND THE REPEAL OF THE PASS LAWS

We, the women of South Africa, have come here today. We represent and we speak on behalf of hundreds of thousands of women who could not be with us. But all over the country, at this moment, women are watching and thinking of us. Their hearts are with us.

We are women from every part of South Africa. We are women of every race. We come from the cities and the towns, from the reserves and the villages. We come as women united in our purpose to save the African women from the degradation of passes.

For hundreds of years the African people have suffered under the most bitter law of all—the pass law which has brought untold suffering to every African family.

Raids, arrests, loss of pay, long hours at the pass office, weeks in the cells awaiting trial, forced farm labour – this is what the pass laws have brought to African men, Punishment and misery – not for a crime, but for the lack of a pass.

We African woman know too well the effect of this law upon our homes, our children. We, who are not African women, know how our sisters suffer.

Your Government proclaims aloud at home and abroad that the pass laws have been abolished, but we women know this is not true, for our husbands, our brothers, our sons are still being arrested, thousands every day, under these very pass laws. It is only the name that has changed. The "reference book" and the pass are one.

In March 1952, your Minister of Native Affairs denied in Parliament that a law would be introduced which would force African women to carry passes. But in 1956 your Government is attempting to force passes upon the African women, and we are here today to protest against this insult to all women. For to us an insult to African women is an insult to all women.

We want to tell you what the pass would mean to an African woman, and we want you to know that whether you call it a reference book, an identity book, or any other disguising name, to us it is a PASS. And it means just this:

- That homes will be broken up when women are arrested under pass laws
- That children will be left uncared for, helpless, and mothers will be torn from their babies for failure to produce a pass
- That women and young girls will be exposed to humiliation and degradation at the hands of pass-searching policemen
- That women will lose their right to move freely from one place to another.

In the name of women of South Africa, we say to you, each one of us, African, European, Indian, Coloured, that we are opposed to the pass system.

We, voters and voteless, call upon your Government not to issue passes to African women.

We shall not rest until ALL pass laws and all forms of permits restricting our freedom have been abolished.

We shall not rest until we have won for our children their fundamental rights of freedom, justice, and security.

NAME_____ADDRESS_____

AREA_____

PRESENTED TO THE PRIME MINISTER
AUGUST 9TH 1956

Appendix 3
MALIBONGWE CONFERENCE:
PROGRAMME OF ACTION (excerpt)

RESOLUTION: WOMEN UNITED

this Malibongwe Conference held on 13–18 January 1990 notes:

- that a serious problem facing women is the lack of strong organisation and structures through which the triple oppression of women can be addressed
- that there is an urgent need for united action towards the formation of a national women's structure
- the necessity to continue within various organisations the process of clarification and discussion of objectives and form (whether alliance, federation, assembly or other) of the new structure
- the need for solidarity among women and between women and men in jointly combatting divisive tendencies, elitism, personaliticals and misconduct in organisations
- the need to forge a working programme that will unite women from various sectors and organisations in a common struggle

THEREFORE RESOLVE TO:

- develop and consolidate our organisations
- broaden existing initiatives and to facilitate discussions in our organisations about the formation of a national women's structure as a priority for building unity in action
- ensure that the issue women's liberation receives priority on the agendas of the ANC and all progressive organisations and that there is an ongoing discussion about the relationship between national liberation, women's liberation and working class victory in these formations
- urge organisations to include women's issues in their political education programmes particularly in the rural areas

- to urge organisations to furmulate and adopt a code of conduct and set up disciplinary structures to address the problems of misconduct, sexual abuse and harassment and exploitative personal relationships
- empower women at all levels within organisations
- urge women to initiate programmes which address community issues, thereby mobilising women and encouraging greater participation.

In conclusion, we, the struggling women of South Africa gathered at this Malibongwe Conference, undertake to implement this Programme of Action in an effort to being closer our objectives of creating a united, non-racial, non-sexist, democratic South Africa

MALIBONGWE IGAMA LAMAKHOSIKAZI

MESSAGE TO POLITICAL TRIALISTS AND PRISONERS

This Malibongwe Conference held in Amsterdam, Netherlands, from 13–18 January 1990 noting the plight of our comrades in apartheid jails for their actions in fighting the apartheid regime and believing that such actions are part of a just cause for the liberation of all South Africans resolved to express solidarity with all comrades awaiting trial or presently on trial and those serving terms of imprisonment.

Appendix 4

SNCC POSITION PAPER
(Women in the Movement)
Name Withheld by Request, November 1964

1. Staff was involved in crucial constitutional revisions at the Atlanta staff meeting in October. A large committee was appointed to present revisions to the staff. The committee was all men.

2. Two organizers were working together to form a farmers league. Without asking any questions, the male organizer immediately assigned the clerical work to the female organizer although both had had equal experience in organizing campaigns.

3. Although there are women in Mississippi project who have been working as long as some of the men, the leadership group in COFO is all men.

4. A woman in a field office wondered why she was held responsible for day to day decisions, only to find out later that she had been appointed project director but not told.

5. A fall 1964 personnel and resources report on Mississippi projects lists the number of people in each project. The section on Laurel, however, lists not the number of persons, but "three girls."

6. One of SNCC's main administrative officers apologizes for appointment of a woman as interim project director in a key Mississippi project area.

7. A veteran of two years' work for SNCC in two states spends her day typing and doing clerical work for other people in her project.

8. Any woman in SNCC, no matter what her position or experience, has been asked to take minutes in a meeting when she and other women are outnumbered by men.

9. The names of several new attorneys entering a state project this past summer were posted in a central movement office. The first initial and last name of each lawyer was listed. Next to one name was written: (girl).

10. Capable, responsible, and experienced women who are in leadership positions can expect to have to defer to a man on their project for final decision making.

11. A session at the recent October staff meeting in Atlanta was the first large meeting in the past couple of years where a woman was asked to chair.

Undoubtedly this list will seem strange to some, petty to others, laughable at most. The list could continue as far as there are women in the movement. Except that most women don't talk about these kinds of incidents, because the whole subject is [not] discussable—strange to some, petty to others, laughable to most. The average white person finds it difficult to understand why the Negro resents being called "boy," or being thought of as "musical" and "athletic," because the average white person doesn't realize that *he assumes he is superior*. And naturally he doesn't understand the problem of paternalism. So too the average SNCC worker finds it difficult to discuss the woman problem because of the assumption of male superiority. Assumptions of male superiority are as widespread and deep rooted and every much as crippling to the woman as the assumptions of white supremacy are to the Negro. Consider why it is in SNCC that women who are competent, qualified, and experienced, are automatically assigned to the "female" kinds of jobs such as typing, desk work, telephone work, filing, library work, cooking, and the assistant kind of administrative work but rarely the "executive" kind.

The woman in SNCC is often in the same position as that token Negro hired in a corporation. The management thinks that it has done its bit. Yet, every day the Negro bears an atmosphere, attitudes and actions which are tinged with condescension and paternalism, the most telling of which are when he is not promoted as the equally or less skilled whites are. This paper is anonymous. Think about the kinds of things the author, if made known, would have to suffer because of raising this kind of discussion. Nothing so final as being fired or outright exclusion, but the kinds of things which are killing to the insides—insinuations, ridicule, over-exaggerated compensations.

This paper is presented anyway because it needs to be made know[n] that many women in the movement are not "happy and contented" with their status. It needs to be made known that much talent and experience are being wasted by this movement when women are not given jobs commensurate with their abilities. It needs to be known that just as Negroes were the crucial factor in the economy of the cotton South, so too in SNCC, women are the crucial factor that keeps the movement running on a day-to-day basis. Yet they are not given equal say-so when it comes to day-to-day decision making. What can be done? Probably nothing right away. Most men in this movement are probably too threatened by the possibility of serious discussion on this subject. Perhaps this is because they have recently broken away from a matriarchal framework under which they may have grown up. Then too, many women are as unaware and insensitive to this subject as men, just as there are many Negroes who don't understand they are not free or who want to be a part of white America. They don't understand that they have to give up their souls and stay in their place to be accepted. So too, many women, in order to be accepted by men, or men's terms, give themselves up to that caricature of what a woman is—unthinking, pliable, an ornament to please the man.

Maybe the only thing that can come out of this paper is discussion—amidst the laughter—but still discussion. (Those who laugh the hardest are often those who need the crutch of male supremacy the most.) And maybe some women will begin to recognize day-to-day discriminations. And maybe sometime in the future the whole of the women in this movement will become so alert as to force the rest of the movement to stop the discrimination and start the slow process of changing values and ideas so that all of us gradually come to understand that this is no more a man's world than it is a white world.

Appendix 5

Black Radical Congress: Principles of Unity

The black radical congress will convene to establish a "center without walls" for transformative politics that will focus on the conditions of Black working and poor people. Recognizing contributions from diverse tendencies within black Radicalism—including socialism, revolutionary nationalism and feminism—we're united in opposition to all forms of oppression, including class exploitation, racism, patriarchy, homophobia, anti-immigration prejudice and imperialism. We will begin with a gathering on June 19–21, 1998. From there we will identify proposals for action and establish paths forward. The Black Radical Congress does not intend to replace or displace existing organizations, parties or campaigns but will contribute to mobilizing unaffiliated individuals, as well as organizations, around common concerns.

1   We recognize the diverse historical tendencies in the Black radical tradition including revolutionary nationalism, feminism and socialism.

2. The technological revolution and capitalist globalization have changed the economy, labor force and class formations that need to inform our analysis and strategies. The increased class polarization created by these developments demands that we, as Black radicals, ally ourselves with the most oppressed sectors of our communities and society.

3. Gender and sexuality can no longer be viewed solely as personal issues by must be a basic part of our analyses, politics and struggles.

4. We reject racial and biological determinism, Black patriarchy and Black capitalism as solutions to problems facing Black people.

5   We must see the struggle in global terms.

6. We need to meet people where they are, taking seriously identity politics and single issue reform groups, at the same time that we push for a larger vision that links these struggles.

7. We must be democratic and inclusive in our dealings with one another, making room for constructive criticism and honest dissent within our ranks. There must be open venues for civil and comradely debates to occur.

8. Our discussions should be informed not only by a critique of what now exists, but by serious efforts to forge a creative vision of new society.

9. We cannot limit ourselves to electoral politics—we must identify multiple sites of struggles.

10. We must overcome divisions within the Black radical forces, such as those of generation, region, and occupation. We must forge a common language that is accessible and relevant.

11. Black radicals must build a national congress of radical forces in the Black community to strengthen radicalism as the legitimate voice of Black working and poor people, and to build organized resistance.

REFERENCES

Ackerman, Peter, and Christopher Kruegler. 1994. *Strategic Nonviolent Conflict: The Dynamics of People Power in the 20th Century*. Westport: Praeger.

Abdulhadi, Rabab. 1998. "The Palestinian Womens' Autonomous Movement Emergence, Dynamics, and Challenges." *Gender and Society* 12(6): 649–73.

Abron, JoNina M. 1998. "'Serving the People': The Survival Programs of the Black Panther Party." Pp. 177–92 in *The Black Panther Party Reconsidered*, ed. Charles E. Jones. Baltimore: Black Classic Press.

Agosin, Marjorie. 1990. *The Mothers of Plaza de Mayo*. Trenton, N.J.: The Red Sea Press, Inc.

Alvarez, Sonia E. 2000. "Translating the Global: Effects of Transnational Organizing on Local Feminist Discourses and Practices in Latin America." *Meridians: Feminism, Race, Transnationalism* 1(1): 29–67.

Aulette, Judy, and Walda Katz Fishman. 1993[1991]. "Working Class Women and the Women's Movement," *Critical Perspectives in Sociology*, 2d ed., ed. Berch Berberoglu. Dubuque: Kendall/Hunt Publishing Company.

Baard, Frances. 1986. *My Spirit Is Not Banned*. Harare: Zimbabwe Publishing House.

Barnes, Teresa. 1997. "'Am I a Man?': Gender and the Pass Laws in Urban Colonial Zimbabwe, 1930–80." *African Studies Review* 40(1): 59–81.

Barnett, Bernice McNair. 1993. "Invisible Southern Black Women Leaders in the Civil Rights Movement: The Triple Constraints of Gender, Race, and Class." *Gender and Society* 7(2): 162–82.

———. 1995. "Black Women's Collectivist Movement Organizations: Their Struggles during the 'Doldrums'." In *Feminist Organizations: Harvest of the New Women's Movement*, ed. Myra Marx Ferree and Patricia Yancey Martin. Philadelphia: Temple University Press.

Basu, Amrita. 2000. "Globalization of the Local/Localization of the Global: Mapping Transnational Women's Movements." *Meridians: Feminism, Race, Transnationalism* 1(1): 68–84.

Beall, Jo, Shireen Hassim, and Alison Todes. 1989. "'A Bit on the Side': Gender Struggles in the Politics of Transformation in South Africa." *Feminist Review* (33): 30–56.

Berger, Iris. 1986. "Sources of Class Consciousness: South African Women in Recent Labor Struggles." Pp. 216–36 in *Women and Class in Africa*, ed. Claire Robertson and Iris Berger. New York: Africana Publishing Company.

———. 1990. "Gender, Race and Political Empowerment: South African Canning Workers, 1940–1960." *Gender and Society* 4(3): 398–420.

Bernstein, Hilda. 1985. *For Their Triumphs and for Their Tears: Women in Apartheid South Africa.* London: International Defence and Aid Fund for Southern Africa.

Bonacich, Edna. 1987. "A Theory of Ethnic Antagonism: The Split Labor Market." *American Sociological Review* 37: 547–59.

Boserup, Ester. 1970. *Women's Role in Economic Development.* New York: St. Martin's Press.

Brewer, Rose M. 1989. "Black Women and Feminist Sociology: The Emerging Perspective." *American Sociologist* 20(1): 57–70.

———. 1993. "Theorizing Race, Class and Gender: The New Scholarship of Black Feminist Intellectuals and Black Women's Labor," Pp. 13–30 in *Theorizing Black Feminisms: The Visionary Pragmatism of Black Women,* ed. Stanlie M. James and Abena P. A. Busia. London: Routledge.

Brown, Elaine. 1992. *A Taste of Power: A Black Woman's Story.* New York: Anchor Books.

Buechler, Steven M. 1993. "Beyond Resource Mobilization? Emerging Trends in Social Movement Theory." *The Sociological Quarterly* 34(2): 217–35.

Cable, Sherry. 1992. "Women's Social Movement Involvement: The Role of Structural Availability in Recruitment and Participation Processes." *The Sociological Quarterly* 33(1): 35–50.

Campbell, Horace. 1997. "The Million Woman March." *Agenda* 34: 86–89.

Cantarow, Ellen, and Susan Bushee O'Malley. 1980. "Ella Baker: Organizing for Civil Rights." Pp. 52–93 in *Moving the Mountain: Women Working for Social Change,* ed. Ellen Cantarow. Old Westbury, N.Y.: The Feminist Press.

Cell, John. 1982. *The Highest Stage of White Supremacy: The Origins of Segregation in South Africa and the American South.* Cambridge: Cambridge University Press.

Cha-Jua, Sundiata Keita. 1998. "The Black Radical Congress and the Reconstruction of the Black Freedom Movement." *The Black Scholar* 28(3/4): 8–21.

Chaney, Elsa M. 1975. "The Mobilization of Women: Three Societies." Pp. 471–87 in *Women Cross-Culturally: Change and Challenge,* ed. Ruby Rohrlich-Leavitt. Paris: Mouton and Co.

Charman, Andrew, Cobus De Swardt, and Mary Simons. 1991. "The Politics of Gender: Negotiating Liberation." *Transformation* 15: 41–64.

Clark, Septima Poinsette. 1986. *Ready from Within: Septima Clark and the Civil Rights Movement.* Navarro, Calif.: Wild Tree.

Cloward, Richard A., and Frances Fox Piven. 1979. "Hidden Protest: The Channeling of Female Innovation and Resistance." *Signs* 4(1): 651–69.

Cole, Josette. 1987. *Crossroads: The Politics of Reform and Repression 1976–1986.* Johannesburg: Ravan Press.

Cohen, Jean. 1985. "Strategy or Identity: New Theoretical Paradigms and Contemporary Social Movements." *Social Research* 52: 663–716.

Collins, Patricia Hill. 2000[1990]. *Black Feminist Thought: Knowledge Consciousness, and the Politics of Empowerment,* 2^d ed. New York: Routledge.

Costain, Anne N. 1992. *Inviting Women's Rebellion: A Political Process Interpretation of the Women's Movement*. Baltimore: The Johns Hopkins University Press.

Craske, Nikki. 1993. "Women's Political Participation in Colonias Populares in Guadalajara, Mexico." Pp. 112–35 in *Viva: Women and Popular Protest in Latin America*, ed. Sarah A. Radcliffe and Sallie Westwood. London: Routledge.

Da Silva Rocha, Filomena. 1988. "Southern African Women and National Liberation Struggles." *Network: A Pan-Africanist Women's Forum* 1(1): 14–18.

Dadzie, Stella. 1990. "Searching for the Invisible Woman: Slavery and Resistance in Jamaica." *Race and Class* 32(2): 21–38.

Davies, Rob, Dan O'Meara, and Sipho Dlamini. 1984. *The Struggle for South Africa: A Reference Guide to Movements, Organizations, and Institutions*, vol. 2. London: Zed Books, Ltd.

Davis, Angela Y. 1981. *Women, Race, and Class*. New York: Vintage Books.

Davis, Miranda, ed. 1983. *Third World–Second Sex: Women's Struggles and National Liberation*. London: Zed Books Limited.

Einwohner, Rachel. 1995. "Gender and Social Movement Outcomes: A Comparison of Two Animal Rights Campaigns." Paper presented at the American Sociological Association, Washington, D.C.

———. 1999. "Gender, Class, and Social Movement Outcomes: Identity and Effectiveness in Two Animal Rights Campaigns." *Gender and Society* 13(1): 56–76.

Einwohner, Rachel L., Jocelyn A. Hollander, and Toska Olson. 2000. "Engendering Social Movements: Cultural Images and Movement Dynamics." *Gender and Society* 14(5): 679–700.

Eisenstein, Hester. 1991. *Gender Shock: Practising Feminism on Two Continents*. North Sydney, Australia: Allen and Unwin Pty Ltd.

Enloe, Cynthia. 1989. *Bananas, Beaches, and Bases: Making Feminist Sense of International Politics*. Berkeley: University of California Press.

Evans, Sara. 1979. *Personal Politics: The Roots of Women's Liberation in the Civil Rights Movement and the New Left*. New York: Alfred A. Knopf.

Federation of South African Women. 1954. "Report of the First National Conference of Women." Bloomington, Ind.: Carter-Karis Collection, Southern African Research Archives Project.

———. 1956a. "Draft Report of the Transvaal Regional Executive Committee of the Federation of South African Women." Bloomington, Ind.: Carter-Karis Collection, Southern African Research Archives Project.

———. 1956b. "Report of the Second National Conference of the Federation of South African Women." Bloomington, Ind.: Carter-Karis Collection, Southern African Research Archives Project.

———. 1958a. "Report by the Federation of South African Women on the Anti-Pass Campaign." Bloomington, Ind.: Carter-Karis Collection, Southern African Research Archives Project.

———. 1958b. "Memorandum on the Pass Laws and the Issuing of Reference Books to African Women submitted by the Federation of South African Women to the Non-European Committee of the City Council of Johannesburg." Bloomington, Ind.: Carter-Karis Collection, Southern African Research Archives Project.

———. n.d. "A Call to Mothers." Bloomington, Ind.: Carter-Karis Collection, Southern African Research Archives Project.

——— (Transvaal Region). n.d. "Women Don't Want Passes." Bloomington, Ind.: Carter-Karis Collection, Southern African Research Archives Project.

Ferree, Myra Marx. 1992. "The Political Context of Rationality: Rational Choice Theory and Resource Mobilization." Pp. 29–52 in *Frontiers in Social Movement Theory*, ed. Aldon Morris and Carol Mueller. New Haven, Conn.: Yale University Press.

Ferree, Myra Marx, and Frederick D. Miller. 1985. "Mobilization and Meaning: Toward an Integration of Social Movements." *Sociological Inquiry* 55: 38–51.

Fester, Gertrude. 1997. "Women's Organizations in the Western Cape: Vehicles for Gender Struggle or Instruments of Subordination?" *Agenda* 34: 45–61.

Fleming, Cynthia Griggs. 1998. *Soon We Will Not Cry*. Lanham, Md.: Rowman and Littlefield Publishers, Inc.

Foner, Philip S. 1995 [1970]. *The Black Panthers Speak*. New York: Da Capo Press, Inc.

Foran, John. 1993. "Theories of Revolution Revisited: Toward a Fourth Generation." *Sociological Theory* 11: 1–20.

Foweraker, Joe. 1995. *Theorizing Socal Movements*. London: Pluto Press.

Fredrickson, George M. 1981. *White Supremacy: A Comparative Study in American and South African History*. Oxford: Oxford University Press.

———. 1995. *Black Liberation: A Comparative History of Black Ideologies in the United States and South Africa*. New York: Oxford University Press.

Freeman, Jo. 1973. "The Origins of the Women's Liberation Movement." *American Journal of Sociology* 78: 792–811.

———. 1979. "Resource Mobilization and Strategy: A Model for Analyzing Social Movement Organization Actions." Pp. 167–89 in *The Dynamics of Social Movements*, ed. Mayer N. Zald and John D. McCarthy. Lanham, Md.: University Press of America.

———. 1993. "Citizenship, Nationality, Gender and Class in Southern Africa." *Alternatives* 18: 39–59.

Gamson, William. 1990 [1975]. *The Strategy of Social Protest*. Belmont: Wadsworth Publishing Company.

Gerson, Judith M., and Kathy Peiss. 1985. "Boundaries, Negotiation, Consciousness: Reconceptualizing Gender Relations." *Social Problems* 32(4): 317–31.

Giddings, Paula. 1984. *When and Where I Enter: The Impact of Black Women on Race and Sex in America*. Toronto: Bantam Books.

Gilliam, Angela. 1991. "Women's Equality and National Liberation." Pp. 215–36 in *Third World Women and the Politics of Feminism*, ed. Chandra Talpade Mohanty, Ann Russo, and Lourdes Torres. Bloomington: Indiana University Press.

Ginsburg, Faye D. 1991. "Gender Politics and the Contradictions of Nurturance: Moral Authority and Constraints to Action for Female Abortion Activist." *Social Research* 58(3): 653–76.

Gluck, Sherna Berger. 1995. "Palestinian Women: Gender Politics and Nationalism." *Journal of Palestine Studies* 24(3): 5–15.

Gurr, Ted Robert. 1970. *Why Men Rebel*. Princeton, N.J.: Princeton University Press.

Hamer, Jennifer, and Helen Neville. 1998. "Revolutionary Black Feminism: Toward a Theory of Unity and Liberation." *The Black Scholar* 28(3/4): 22–29.

Hassim, Shireen. 1993. "Family, Motherhood, and Zulu Nationalism: The Politics of the Inkatha Women's Brigade." *Feminist Review* (43): 1–25.

Hess, Beth B., and Myra Marx Ferree, eds. 1987. *Analyzing Gender: A Handbook of Social Science*. Newbury Park, Calif.: Sage.

hooks, bell. 1981. *Ain't I a Woman: Black Women and Feminism*. Boston: South End Press.

———. 1984. *Feminist Theory: From Margin to Center*. Boston: South End Press.

James, Joy. 1999. *Shadowboxing: Representations of Black Feminist Politics*. New York: St. Martin's Press.

———. 2000. "Resting in Gardens, Battling in Deserts: Black Women's Activism." *The Black Scholar* 29(4): 2–7.

Jaquette, Jane S. 1994. *The Women's Movement in Latin America: Participation and Democracy*. Boulder, Colo.: Westview Press.

Jayawardena, Kumari. 1986. *Feminism and Nationalism in the Third World*. London: Zed Books Ltd.

Jeffery, Anthea. 1991. *Forum on Mass Mobilization*. Johannesburg: South African Institute of Race Relations.

Jenkins, Craig J., and Charles Perrow. 1977. "Insurgency of the Powerless: Farm Worker Movements (1946–72)." *American Sociological Review* 42(2): 249–68.

Johnson-Odim, Cheryl, and Nina Emma Mba. 1997. *For Women and the Nation: Funmilayo Ransome-Kuti of Nigeria*. Urbana, Ill.: University of Illinois Press.

Johnston, Hank, Enrique Larana, and Joseph R. Gusfield. 1997. "Identities, Grievances, and New Social Movements." Pp. 274–95 in *Social Movements: Perspectives and Issues*, ed. Stephen Buechler and F. Kurt Cylke Jr. Mountain View, Calif.: Mayfield Publishing Company.

Kaplan, Temma. 1990. "Community and Resistance in Women's Political Cultures." *Dialectical Anthropology* 15: 259–67.

Kemp, Amanda, Nozizwe Madlala, Asha Moodley, and Elaine Salo. 1995. "The Dawn of a New Day: Redefining South African Feminism." Pp. 131–62 in *The Challenge of Local Feminisms: Women's Movements in Global Perspective*. Boulder, Colo.: Westview Press.

Kimble, Judy, and Elaine Unterhalter. 1982. "'We Opened the Road for You, You Must Go Forward': ANC Women's Struggles, 1912–1982." *Feminist Review* (12): 11–33.

King, Deborah. 1988. "Multiple Jeopardy, Multiple Consciousness: The Context of a Black Feminist Ideology." *Signs* 14(1): 42–72.

Klandermans, Bert. 1984. "Mobilization and Participation: Social-Psychological Expansions of Resource Mobilization Theory." *American Sociological Review* 49: 583–600.

———. 1986. "New Social Movements and Resource Mobilization: The European and American Approach." *International Journal of Mass Emergencies and Disasters* 4: 13–37.

Kuumba, M. Bahati. 1999. "Engendering the Pan-African Movement: Field Notes from the All-African Women's Revolutionary Union." Pp. 167–88 in *Still Lifting, Still Climbing: African American Women's Contemporary Activism*, ed. Kimberly Springer. New York: New York University Press.

Kuumba, M. Bahati, and Ona Alston-Dosunmu. 1995. "Women in National Liberation Struggles in the Third World," Pp. 95–130 in *The National Question: Nationalism, Ethnic Conflict and Self-Determination in the 20th Century*, ed. Berch Berberoglu. Philadelphia: Temple University Press.

La Hausse, Paul. 1988. *Brewers, Beerhalls and Boycotts: A History of Liquor in South Africa*. Johannesburg: Ravan Press.

Landis, Elizabeth. 1982. "African Women under Apartheid." Pp. 1–4 in *Resistance, War and Liberation: Women of Southern Africa*. New York: Women's International Resource Exchange.

Lapchick, Richard E. 1981. "The Role of Women in the Struggle against Apartheid in South Africa." In *The Black Woman Cross-Culturally*, ed. Filomina Chioma Steady. Rochester, Vt.: Schenkman Books, Inc.

Lapchick, Richard E., and Stephanie Urdang. 1982. *Oppression and Resistance: The Struggle of Women in Southern Africa*. Westport, Conn.: Greenwood Press.

Lawson, Ronald, and Stephen E. Barton. 1980. "Sex Roles in Social Movements: A Case Study of the Tenant Movement in New York City." *Signs* 6(2): 230–47.

LeBlanc-Ernest, Angela D. 1998. "'The Most Qualified Person to Handle the Job': Black Panther Party Women, 1966–1982." Pp. 305–34 in *The Black Panther Party Reconsidered*, ed. Charles E. Jones. Baltimore: Black Classic Press.

Lobao, Linda. 1990. "Women in Revolutionary Movements: Changing Patterns of Latin American Guerrilla Struggle." Pp. 180–204 in *Women and Social Protest*, ed. Guida West and Rhoda Lois Blumberg. New York: Oxford Press.

Lodge, Tom. 1984. *Black Politics in South Africa since 1945*. London: Longman.

Lofland, John. 1996. *Social Movement Organizations: Guide to Research on Insurgent Realities*. New York: Aldine De Gruyter.

Lopata, Helena, and Barrie Thorne. 1978. "On the Term 'Sex Roles.'" *Signs* 3: 718–21.

Lorber, Judith. 1997[1993]. "'Night to His Day': The Social Construction of Gender." Pp. 33–47 in *Feminist Frontiers IV*, ed. Laurel Richardson, Verta Taylor, and Nancy Whittier. New York: McGraw-Hill.

Lourde, Audre. 1984. *Sister Outsider*. Freedom, Calif.: The Crossing Press.

Lunn, Helen, ed. 1983[1955]. "Education Shebeens." Pp. 126–28 in *The Beat of the Drum*, vol. 2, ed. Helen Lunn. Southern Africa: J.R.A. Bailey.

Lusane, Clarence. 1997. *Race in the Global Era: African Americans at the Millennium*. Boston: South End Press.

Machel, Samora. 1980. "Women's Liberation is Essential for the Revolution." Pp. 157–68 in *Revolutionary Thought in the 20th Century*, ed. Ben Turok. London: Zed Press Limited.

MacQuene, Althea. 1996. *Weaving Gender into Our Work: A Handbook for Working People and Their Organizations*. Salt River, South Africa: International Labour Resource and Information Group.

Magubane, Bernard Makhosezwe. 1979. *The Political Economy of Race and Class in South Africa*. New York: Monthly Review Press.

Malahleha, G. M. 1985. "Liquor Brewing: A Cottage Industry in Lesotho Shebeens." *Journal of Eastern African Research and Development* 15: 45–55.

Marcus, Tessa. 1988. "The Women's Question and National Liberation in South Africa." Pp. 96–109 in *The National Questions in South Africa*, ed. Maria van Diepen. London: Zed Books Ltd.

Marger, Martin. 1997. *Race and Ethnic Relations: American and Global Perspectives*. Belmont, Calif.: Wadsworth Publishing Company.

Marx, Gary T. 1982. "External Efforts to Damage or Facilitate Social Movements: Some Patterns, Explanations, Outcomes, and Complications." Pp. 181–200 in *Social Movements: Development, Participation, and Dynamics*, ed. James L. Wood and Maurice Jackson. Belmont, Calif.: Wadsworth Publishing Company.

Mashinini, Emma. 1991. *Strikes Have Followed Me All My Life*. New York: Routledge.

Matthews, Tracye. 1998. "'No One Ever Asks, What a Man's Place in the Revolution Is': Gender and the Politics of the Black Panther Party." Pp. 267-304 in *The Black Panther Party Reconsidered*, ed. Charles E. Jones. Baltimore: Black Classic Press.

McAdam, Doug. 1982. *Political Process and the Development of Black Insurgency 1930– 1970*. Chicago: The University of Chicago Press.

———. 1983. "Tactical Innovation and the Pace of Insurgency." *American Sociological Review* 48: 735–54.

———. 1992. "Gender as a Mediator of the Activist Experience: The Case of Freedom Summer." *American Journal of Sociology* 97(5): 1211–40.

McAllister, Pam. 1991. *This River of Courage: Generations of Women's Resistance and Action*. Philadelphia: New Society Publishers.

McCarthy, John D., and Zald, Mayer N. 1977. "Resource Mobilization and Social Movements: A Partial Theory." *American Journal of Sociology* 82(6): 1212–41.

McFadden, Patricia. 1992. "Nationalism and Gender Issues in South Africa." *Journal of Gender Studies* 1(4): 510–20.

Meena, Ruth, ed. 1992. *Gender in Southern Africa: Conceptual and Theoretical Issues*. Harare: SAPES Books.

Meer, Fatima. 1985. "Women in the Apartheid Society." ANC Notes and Documents 4(85).

Meer, Shamin. 1998. *Women Speak: Reflections on Our Struggles, 1982–1997*. Cape Town: Kwela Books.

Meintjes, Sheila. 1998. "Gender, Nationalism and Transformation: Difference and Commonality in South Africa's Past and Present." Pp. 62–86 in *Women, Ethnicity and Nationalism: The Politics of Transition*, ed. Rick Wilford and Robert L. Miller. London: Routledge.

Melucci, Alberto. 1985. "The Symbolic Challenge of Contemporary Movements." *Social Research* 52: 789–816.

Meier, August, and Elliot Rudwick. 1973. *CORE: A Study in the Civil Rights Movement, 1942–1968*. New York: Oxford University Press.

Mies, Maria. 1986. *Patriarchy and Accumulation on a World Scale*. London: Zed Books, Ltd.

Minkoff, Debra. 1993. "Shaping Contemporary Organizational Action: Women's and Minority Social Change Strategies, 1955–85." Paper presented at the American Sociological Association Meetings, Miami, Florida.

Molyneux, Maxine. 1985. "Mobilization Without Emancipation? Women's Interests, State, and Revolution." *Feminist Studies* 11: 227–54.

Morris, Aldon D. 1984. *The Origins of the Civil Rights Movement: Black Communities Organizing for Change*. New York: The Free Press.

Moya-Raggio, Eliana. 1984. "Arpilleras: Chilean Culture of Resistance." *Feminist Studies* 10(2): 277–90.

Naples, Nancy A., ed. 1998. *Community Activism and Feminist Politics: Organizing across Race, Class, and Gender*. New York: Routledge.

Nauright, John. 1996. "'I Am with You as Never Before': Women in Urban Protest Movements, Alexandra Townships, South Africa, 1912–1945." Pp. 259–83 in *Courtyards, Markets, City Streets: Urban Women in Africa*, ed. Kathleen Sheldon. Boulder, Colo.: Westview Press.

Neuhouser, Kevin. 1995. "'Worse than Men': Gendered Mobilization in an Urban Brazilian Squatter Settlement, 1971–91." *Gender and Society* 9(1): 38–59.

Noonan, Rita K. 1995. "Women against the State: Political Opportunities and Collective Action Frames in Chile's Transition to Democracy." *Sociological Forum* 10(1): 81–111.

Payne, Charles. 1990. "Men Led, But Women Organized: Movement Participation of Women in the Mississippi Delta." In *Women and Social Protest*, ed. Guida West and Rhoda Lois Blumberg. New York: Oxford University Press.

———. 1995. *I've Got the Light of Freedom: The Organizing Tradition and the Mississippi Freedom Struggle.* Berkeley: University of California Press.

Peterson, V. Spike. 1994. "Gendered Nationalism." *Peace Review* 6(1): 77–83.

Peterson, V. Spike, and Anne Sisson Runyan. 1999. *Global Gender Issues*, 2ᵈ ed. Boulder, Colo.: Westview Press.

Pfaff, Steven. 1996. "Collective Identity and Informal Groups in Revolutionary Mobilization: East Germany in 1989." *Social Forces* 75(1): 91–118.

Piven, Frances Fox, and Richard A. Cloward. 1979. *Poor People's Movements: Why They Succeed and How They Fail.* New York: Vintage Books.

Platt, Gerald M., and Michael R. Fraser. 1998. "Race and Gender Discourse Strategies: Creating Solidarity and Framing the Civil Rights Movement." *Social Problems* 45(2): 160–79.

Primo, Natasha. 1997. "Women's Emancipation: Resistance and Empowerment." *Agenda* 34: 31–44.

Ramphele, Mamphela. 1991. "The Dynamics of Gender within Black Consciousness Organizations: A Personal View." Pp. 214–27 in *Bounds of Possibilities: The Legacy of Steve Biko and Black Consciousness*, ed. N. Barney Pityana, Mamphela Ramphele, Malusi Mpumlwana, and Lindy Wilson. Cape Town: David Philip.

Randall, Margaret. 1981. *Sandino's Daughters: Testimonies of Nicaraguan Women in Struggle.* Vancouver and Toronto: New Star Books.

Ray, Raka. 1999. *Fields of Protest: Women's Movements in India.* Minneapolis: University of Minnesota Press.

Reagon, Bernice Johnson. 1979. "My Black Mothers and Sisters . . ." and "Question and Answer Session: Women and the Black Liberation Struggle." Conference Proceedings: Black Women and Liberation Movements. Howard University, Washington, D.C., November 8.

———. 1981. "Ella's Song." *Breaths* (album sung by Sweet Honey in the Rock). Songtalk Publishing Company.

———. 1993a. "Battle Stancing: To Do Cultural Work in America." Pp. 69–82 in *Voices from the Battlefront: Achieving Cultural Equity*, ed. Marta I. Moreno Vega and Cheryll Y. Greene. Trenton, N.J.: Africa World Press.

———. 1993b. "Women as Culture Carriers in the Civil Rights Movement: Fannie Lou Hamer." Pp. 203–18 in *Women in the Civil Rights Movement, Trailblazers and Torchbearers: 1941–1965*, ed. Vicki L. Crawford, Jacqueline Anne Rouse, and Barbara Woods. Bloomington: Indiana University Press.

Robinson, Jo Ann Gibson. 1987. *The Montgomery Bus Boycott and the Women Who Started It.* Knoxville: The University of Tennessee Press.

Robnett, Belinda. 1996. "African American Women in the Civil Rights Movement, 1954–1965: Gender, Leadership, and Micromobilization." *American Journal of Sociology* 101(6): 1661–93.

———. 1997. *How Long? How Long? African-American Women in the Struggle for Civil Rights.* New York: Oxford University Press.

Rodriguez, Lilia. 1994. "Barrio Women: Between the Urban and Feminist Movement." *Latin American Perspectives* 21(3): 32–48.

Rowbotham, Sheila. 1992. *Women in Movement: Feminism and Social Action.* London: Routledge.

Sachs, Karen. 1988. *Caring by the Hour: Women, Work, and Organizing at Duke Medical Center.* Urbana: University of Illinois Press.

Sankara, Thomas. 1988. "The Revolution Cannot Triumph without the Emancipation of Women." Pp. 201–27 in *Thomas Sankara Speaks: The Burkina Faso Revolution 1983–87,* trans. Samantha Anderson. New York: Pathfinder Press.

Schild, Veronica. 1994. "Recasting 'Popular' Movements: Gender and Political Learning in Neighborhood Organizations in Chile." *Latin American Perspectives* 21(2): 59–80.

Schirmer, Jennifer. 1993. "The Seeking of Truth and the Gendering of Consciousness." Pp. 30–64 in *Viva: Women and Popular Protest in Latin America,* ed. Sarah A. Radcliffe and Sallie Westwood. London: Routledge.

Scott, James C. 1985. *Weapons of the Weak: Everyday Forms of Peasant Resistance.* New Haven: Yale University Press.

———. 1995. *Domination and the Arts of Resistance: Hidden Transcripts.* New Haven, Conn.: Yale University Press.

Seager, Joni. 1997. *The State of Women in the World Atlas.* Middlesex, England: Penguin Books Limited.

Seale, Bobby. 1970. *Seize the Time: The Story of the Black Panther Party and Huey P. Newton.* Baltimore: Black Classic Press.

Seidman, Gay. 1993. "'No Freedom without the Women': Mobilization and Gender in South Africa, 1970–1992." *Signs* 18(2): 291–320.

———. 1994. *Manufacturing Militance: Worker's Movements in Brazil and South Africa.* Berkeley: University of California Press.

Shapiro-Perl, Nina. 1984. "Resistance Strategies: The Routine Struggle for Bread and Roses," Pp. 193–208 in *My Troubles Are Going to Have Trouble with Me: Everyday Trials and Triumphs of Women Workers,* ed. Karen Brodkin Sachs and Dorothy Remy. New Brunswick, N.J.: Rutgers University Press.

Sharoni, Simona. 1995a. *Gender and the Israeli-Palestinian Conflict: The Politics of Women's Resistance.* Syracuse: Syracuse University Press.

———. 1995b. "Gendered Identities in Conflict: The Israeli-Palestinian Case and Beyond." *Women's Studies Quarterly* 23(3/4): 117–35.

Sinha, Mrinalini, Donna Guy, and Angela Woollacott, eds. 1999. *Feminisms and Internationalism.* Oxford: Blackwell Publishers.

Smelser, Neil. 1962. *Theory of Collective Behavior.* New York: Free Press.

Snow, David A., and Robert D. Benford. 1988. "Ideology, Frame Resonance, and Participant Mobilization." *International Social Movement Research* 1: 197–217.

———. 1992. "Master Frames and Cycles of Protest." Pp. 133–55 in *Frontiers in Social Movement Theory,* ed. Aldon D. Morris and Carol McClurg Mueller. New Haven, Conn.: Yale University Press.

Snow, David A., E. Burke Rochford Jr., Steven K. Worden, and Robert D. Benford. 1986. "Frame Alignment Processes, Micromobilization, and Movement Participation." *American Sociological Review* 51: 464–81.

Snow, David A., Louis A. Zurcher, and Sheldon Elkand-Olson. 1980. "Social Networks and Social Movements: A Microstructural Approach to Differential Recruitment." *American Sociological Review* 45: 787–801.

Springer, Kimberly. 1999. *Still Lifting, Still Climbing: African American Women's Contemporary Activism.* New York: New York University Press.

———. 2001. "The Interstitial Politics of Black Feminist Organizations." *Meridians: Feminism, Race, Transnationalism* 1(2): 155–91.

Staples, Robert. 1979. "The Myth of Black Macho: A Response to Angry Black Feminists." *The Black Scholar* 10(8): 24–33.

Stacey, Judith, and Barrie Thorne. 1985. "The Missing Feminist Revolution in Sociology." *Social Problems* 32(4): 301–16.

Steady, Filomina Chioma. 1985 [1981]. *The Black Woman Cross-Culturally.* Rochester: Vt.: Schenkman Books, Inc.

Stotik, Jeffrey, Thomas E. Shriver, and Sherry Cable. 1994. "Social Control and Movement Outcome: The Case of AIM." *Sociological Focus* 27(1): 53–66.

Tarrow, Sidney. 1995. "Cycles of Collective Action: Between Moments of Madness and the Repertoire of Contention." Pp. 89–115 in *Repertoires and Cycles of Collective Action*, ed. Mark Traugott. Durham, N.C.: Duke University Press.

Taylor, Verta. 1995. "Watching for Vibes: Bringing Emotions into the Study of Feminist Organizations." Pp. 223–33 in *Feminist Organizations: Harvest of the New Women's Movement*, ed. Myra Marx Ferree and Patricia Yancey Martin. Philadelphia: Temple University Press.

———. 1999. "Gender and Social Movements." *Gender and Society* 13(1): 1–8.

Taylor, Verta, and Nancy Whittier. 1992. "Collective Identity in Social Movements: Lesbian Feminist Mobilization." Pp. 104–30 in *Frontiers in Social Movement Theory*, ed. Aldon D. Morris and Carol McClurg Mueller. New Haven, Conn.: Yale University Press.

———. 1999. "Guest Editors' Introduction: Special Issue on Gender and Social Movements: Part 2." *Gender and Society* 13(1): 5–7.

Taylor, Viviene. 1997. *Social Mobilization: Lessons from the Mass Democratic Movement.* Bellville, South Africa: University of the Western Cape.

Terborg-Penn, Rosalyn. 1990. "Black Women Freedom Fighters in South Africa and in the United States: A Comparative Analysis." *Dialectical Anthropology* 15: 151–57.

United States Commission on Civil Rights. 1990. *The Economic Status of Black Women: An Exploratory Investigation.* Washington, D.C.: U.S. Government Printing Office.

Vukani Makhosikazi Collective. 1985. *South African Women in the Move.* London: Catholic Institute for International Relations.

Walker, Cherryl. 1982. *Women and Resistance in South Africa.* London: Onyx Press.

———. 1995. "Conceptualizing Motherhood in Twentieth Century South Africa." *Journal of Southern African Studies* 21(3): 417–37.

Wells, Julia C. 1993. *We Now Demand! The History of Women's Resistance to the Pass Laws in South Africa.* Johannesburg: Witwatersrand University Press.

West, Guida and Rhoda Lois Blumberg. 1990. "Reconstructing Social Protest from a Feminist Perspective." Pp. 3–35 in *Women and Social Protest*, ed. Guida West and Rhoda Lois Blumberg. New York: Oxford University Press.

Westwood, Sally, and Sarah A. Radcliffe. 1993. "Gender, Racism and the Politics of Identities in Latin America." Pp. 1–29 in *Viva: Women and Popular Protest in Latin America*, ed. Sarah A. Radcliffe and Sallie Westwood. London: Routledge.

Wolphe, Harold. 1990. *Race, Class, and the Apartheid State*. Trenton, N.J.: Africa World Press.

Women's International Resource Exchange (WIRE). 1982. *Resistance, War and Liberation: Women of Southern Africa*. New York: Women's International Resource Exchange.

Women's National Coalition. 1994. "The Origins, History and the Process of the Women's National Coalition." Marshalltown, South Africa: WNC.

Wood, James L., and Maurice Jackson. 1982. *Social Movements: Development, Participation, and Dynamics*. Belmont: Wadsworth Publishing Company.

Younis, Mona N. 2000. *Liberation and Democratization: The South African and Palestinian National Movements*. Minneapolis: University of Minnesota.

Zinn, Howard. 1964. *SNCC: The New Abolitionists*. Boston: Beacon Press.

Further Reading

Abdo, Nahla. 1991. "Women of the Intifada: Gender, Class, and National Liberation." *Race and Class* 32(4):19–34.

Afshar, Haleh. 1996. *Women and Politics in the Third World*. London: Routledge.

Albrecht, Lisa, and Rose Brewer, eds. 1990. *Bridges of Power: Women's Multicultural Alliances*. Santa Cruz: New Society Publishers.

Alvarez, Sonia E. 1990. *Engendering Democracy in Brazil: Women's Movements in Transition Politics*. Princeton: Princeton University Press.

Anthias, Floya, and Nira Yuval-Davis. 1983. "Contextualizing Feminism—Gender, Ethnic and Class Divisions." *Feminist Review* 15: 62–74.

———. 1989. "Introduction." Pp. 1–15 in *Woman-Nation-State*, ed. Floya Anthias and Nira Yuval-Davis. London: The MacMillan Press Ltd.

Bahl, Vinay. 1989. "Women in the Third World: Problems in Proletarianization and Class Consciousness." *Sage Race Relations Abstracts* 14(2): 3–26.

Bair, Barbara. 1992. "True Women, Real Men: Gender, Ideology, and Social Roles in the Garvey Movement." *Gendered Domains: Rethinking Public and Private in Women's History*, ed. Dorothy O. Helly and Susan M. Reverby. Ithaca: Cornell University Press.

Barnett, Bernice McNair. Forthcoming. *Sisters in Struggle: Invisible Black Women Leaders of the Civil Rights Movement, 1945–1975*. New York: Routledge.

Bem, Sandra Lipsitz. 1993. *The Lenses of Gender: Transforming the Debate on Sexual Inequality*. New Haven, Conn.: Yale University Press.

Benallegue, Nora. 1983. "Algerian Women in the Struggle for Independence and Reconstruction." *International Social Science Journal* 35(4): 703–17.

Bernard, Jessie. 1987. *The Female World from a Global Perspective*. Bloomington: Indiana University Press.

Blumberg, Rhoda Lois. 1990. "Women in the Civil Rights Movement: Reform or Revolution." *Dialectical Anthropology* 15: 133–39.

Booth, Alan. 1972. "Sex and Social Participation." *American Sociological Review* 37(2): 183–93.

Bozzoli, Belinda. 1991. *Women of Phokeng: Consciousness, Life Strategy, and Migrancy in South Africa, 1900–1983*. Portsmouth, N.H.: Heinemann.

Buechler, Steven M., and F. Kurt Cylke Jr. 1997. *Social Movements Perspectives and Issues*. Mountain View, Calif.: Mayfield Publishing Company.

Bush, Rod. 1998. *We Are Not What We Seem: Black Nationalism and the Class Struggle in the American Century.* New York: New York University Press.

Bystydzienski, Jill M., ed. 1992. *Women Transforming Politics: Worldwide Strategies for Empowerment.* Bloomington: Indiana University Press.

Cable, Sherry, Edward J. Walsh, and Rex H. Warland. 1988. "Differential Paths to Political Activism: Comparisons of Four Mobilization Processes after the Three Mile Island Accident." *Social Forces* 66(4): 951–69.

Calhoun, Craig. 1991. "The Problem of Identity in Collective Action." Pp. 51–75 in *Macro-Micro Linkages in Sociology,* ed. Joan Huber. Thousand Oaks, Calif.: Sage.

Carmichael, Stokely (Kwame Ture), and Charles V. Hamilton. 1967. *Black Power: The Politics of Liberation in America.* New York: Random House.

Carter, Gwendolyn M. 1979. "South Africa: Growing Black-White Confrontation." Pp. 93–140 in *Southern Africa: The Continuing Crisis,* ed. Gwendolyn M. Carter and Patrick O'Meara. Bloomington: Indiana University Press.

Casaburri, Ivy Matsepe. 1986. "On the Question of Women in the South African Struggle." *African Journal of Political Economy* 1: 40–59.

Chafetz, Janet Saltzman. 1986. *Female Revolt: Women's Movements in World and Historical Perspective.* Toitowa, N.J.: Rowman and Allenheld.

Chatterjee, Partha. 1989. "Colonialism, Nationalism, and Colonialized Women: The Contest in India." *American Ethnologist* 16: 622–33.

Clara. 1989. "Feminism and the Struggle for National Liberation." *The African Communist* 118: 38–43.

Cleaver, Kathleen Neal. 1993. "Sister Act: Symbol and Substance in Black Women's Leadership." *Transition: An International Review* 60: 84–100.

Cleaver Tessa, and Marion Wallace. 1990. *Namibian Women in War.* London: Zed Books Limited.

Cock, Jacklyn. 1993. *Women and War in South Africa.* Cleveland: The Pilgrim Press.

The Commission on Gender Equality. 1998. *Annual Report of the Commission on Gender Equality.* Johannesburg: CGE.

Committees on the Status of Women in Sociology. 1986. *The Treatment of Gender in Research.* Washington, D.C.: American Sociological Association.

Crawford, Vicki L., Jacqueline Anne Rouse, and Barbara Woods. 1990. *Women in the Civil Rights Movement: Trailblazers and Torchbearers, 1941–1965.* Bloomington: Indiana University Press.

Danforth, Sandra C. 1984. "The Social and Political Implications of Muslim Middle Eastern Women's Participation in Violent Political Conflict." *Women and Politics* 4(1): 35–54.

Davenport, T. R. H. 1991[1977]. *South Africa: A Modern History.* Toronto: University of Toronto Press.

Davies, James. 1962. "Towards a Theory of Revolution." *American Sociological Review* 27: 5–19.

Davis, Angela Y. 1971. "Reflections on the Black Woman's Role in the Community of Slaves." *The Black Scholar* (December): 3–15.

———. 1990. *Women, Culture, and Politics.* New York: Vintage Books.

Davis, Miranda, ed. 1987. *Third World–Second Sex, Volume 2.* London: Zed Books Limited.

Eder, Klaus. 1985. "The 'New Social Movements': Moral Crusades, Political Pressure Groups, or Social Movements." *Social Research* 52: 869–90.

Escobar, Arturo, and Sonia E. Alvarez, eds. 1992. *The Making of Social Movements in Latin America: Identity, Strategy, and Democracy.* Boulder, Colo.: Westview Press.

Federation of South African Women. 1958. "Report by the Federation of S.A. Women on the Anti-Pass Campaign." Carter-Karis Collection, Southern African Research Archives Project, Bloomington, Ind.

Fleming, Cynthia Griggs. 1995. "Black Women Activists and the Student Nonviolent Coordinating Committee: The Case of Ruby Doris Smith Robinson." Pp. 561–77 in *We Specialize in the Wholly Impossible: A Reader in Black Women's History*, ed. Darlene Clark Hine, Wilma King, and Linda Reed. New York: Carlson Publishing, Inc.

Fisher, Jo. 1993. *Out of the Shadows: Women, Resistance and Politics in South America.* London: Latin American Bureau.

Foner, Philip S. 1995[1970]. *The Black Panthers Speak.* New York: Da Capo Press.

Frates, L. Lloyd. 1993. "Women in the South African National Liberation Movement, 1948–1960: An Historiographical Overview." *Ufahamu: Journal of the Africanist Association* 21(1/2): 27–40.

Friedman, Debra, and Doug McAdam. 1992. "Collective Identity and Activism: Networks, Choices, and the Life of a Social Movement." Pp. 156–73 in *Frontiers in Social Movement Theory*, ed. Aldon Morris and Carol McClurg Mueller. New Haven, Conn.: Yale University Press.

Gaidzanwa, Rudo. 1988. "Feminism: The Struggle within the Struggle." *Network: A Pan-African Women's Forum* 1(1): 4–13.

Gaitskell, Deborah, and Elaine Unterhalter. 1989. "Mothers of the Nation: A Comparative Analysis of Nation, Race and Motherhood in Afrikaner Nationalism and the African National Congress." Pp. 58–78 in *Woman-Nation-State*, ed. Floya Anthias and Nira Yuval-Davis. London: The MacMillan Press Ltd.

Gallin, Rita S., and Anne Ferguson. 1991. "Introduction: Conceptualizing Difference: Gender, Class, and Action." Pp. 1–30 in *The Women and International Development Annual*, vol. 2, ed. Rita S. Gallin and Anne Ferguson. Boulder, Colo.: Westview Press.

Geiger, Susan. 1987. "Women in Nationalist Struggle: TANU Activists in Dar Es Salaam." *The International Journal of African Historical Studies* 20(1): 1–26.

Gibson, Richard. 1972. *African Liberation Movements: Contemporary Struggles against White Minority Rule.* London: Oxford University Press.

Gilkes, Cheryl Townsend. 1988. "Building in Many Places: Multiple Commitments and Ideologies in Black Women's Community Work." Pp. 53–76 in *Women and the Politics of Empowerment*, ed. Ann Bookman and Sandra Morgen. Philadelphia: Temple University Press.

Goodwin, Jeff. 1994. "Toward a New Sociology of Revolutions." *Theory and Society* 23: 731–66.

Goodwin, June. 1984. *Cry Amandla! South African Women and the Question of Power.* New York: Africana Publishing Company.

Gould, Roger V.. 1991. "Multiple Networks and Mobilization in the Paris Commune." *American Sociological Review* 56: 716–29.

Grant, Joanne. 1998. *Ella Baker: Freedom Bound*. New York: John Wiley and Sons, Inc.

Guy-Sheftall, Beverly. 1995. *Words of Fire: An Anthology of African-American Feminist Thought*. New York: The New Press.

Gyant, LaVerne. 1996. "Passing the Torch: African American Women in the Civil Rights Movement." *Journal of Black Studies* 26(5): 629–47.

Habtemariam, Tsehai. 1990. "The Eritrean Woman after Independence." Pp. 79–86 in *Proceedings of the International Conference on Eritrea, November 3–4, 1990 in Baltimore Maryland*. Washington, D.C.: Eritreans for Peace and Democracy.

Hammond, Jenny, and Neil Druce. 1990. *Sweeter Than Honey—Ethiopian Women and Revolution: Testimonies of Tigrayan Women*. Trenton, N.J.: The Red Sea Press, Inc.

Hartstock, Nancy. 1985. "Exchange Theory: Critique from a Feminist Standpoint." Pp. 57–70 in *Current Perspectives in Social Theory*, vol. 6, ed. Scott McNall. Greenwich, Conn.: JAI.

Hassim, Shireen. 1991. "Gender, Social Location and Feminist Politics in South Africa." *Transformation* 15: 65–82.

———. 1999. "From Presence to Power: Women's Citizenship in a New Democracy." *Agenda* 40: 6–17.

Hassim, Shireen, and Cherryl Walker. 1993. "Women's Studies and the Women's Movement in South Africa—Defining a Relationship." *Women's Studies International Forum* 6(5): 423–34.

Hawkesworth, Mary. 1997. "Confounding Gender." *Signs: Journal of Women in Culture and Society* 22(3): 649–85.

Hertz, Susan H. 1977. "The Politics of the Welfare Mothers Movement: A Case Study." *Signs* 2(3): 600–11.

Hiltermann, Joost R. 1991. *Behind the Intifada: Labor and Women's Movements in the Occupied Territories*. Princeton, N.J.: Princeton University Press.

Hindson, Doug. 1987. *Pass Controls and the Urban African Proletariat*. Johannesburg: Raven Press.

Hirsch, Eric L. 1990. "Sacrifice for the Cause: Group Processes, Recruitment, and Commitment in a Student Social Movement." *American Sociological Review* 55: 243–54.

Holland, Heidi. 1989. *The Struggle: A History of the African National Congress*. London: Grafton Books.

Holness, Marga. 1984. *Angolan Women: Building the Future*. London: Zed Books, Ltd.

Horn, Patricia. 1991. "Conference on Women and Gender in Southern Africa: Another View of the Dynamics." *Transformation* (15): 83–88.

Howard, Judy A., and Jocelyn Hollander. 1997. *Gendered Situations, Gendered Selves*. Thousand Oaks, Calif.: Sage Publications.

International Defence and Aid Fund for Southern Africa. 1981. *Women Under Apartheid: In Photographs and Text*. London: United Nations Center Against Apartheid.

International Defence and Aid Fund. 1980. *You Have Struck a Rock: Women and Political Repression in Southern Africa*. London: International Defence and Aid Fund.

Irons, Jenny. 1998. "The Shaping of Activist Recruitment and Participation: A Study of Women in the Mississippi Civil Rights Movement." *Gender and Society* 12(6): 692–709.

James, Joy. 1994. "Ella Baker, Black Women's Work and Activist Intellectuals." *The Black Scholar* 24(8): 8–15.

Jaquette, Jane, ed. 1989. *The Women's Movement in Latin America: Feminism and the Transition to Democracy.* Winchester, Mass.: Unwin Hyman.

Jenkins, J. Craig. 1983. "Resource Mobilization Theory and the Study of Social Movements." *Annual Review of Sociology* 9: 527–53.

Jirira, Kwanele Ona. 1989. "Women in Zimbabwe: Coming Out of Men's Political Shadows." *Southern Africa Political and Economic Monthly* 3(1): 32–35.

Johnson-Odim, Cheryl. 1991. "Common Themes, Different Contexts: Third World Women and Feminism." Pp. 314–27 in *Third World Women and the Politics of Feminism*, ed. Chandra Talpade Mohanty, Ann Russo, and Lourdes Torres. Bloomington: Indiana University Press.

Jolly, Margaret. 1994. "Motherlands? Some Notes on Women and Nationalism in India and Africa." *The Australian Journal of Anthropology* 5(1/2): 41–59.

Joseph, Helen. 1956. "Women Against Passes." In *Fighting Talk*. Federation of South African Women (April): 3–4.

Kaplan, Temma. 1997. *Crazy for Democracy: Women in Grassroots Movements*. New York: Routledge.

Kling, Susan. 1982. "Fannie Lou Hamer: Baptism by Fire." Pp. 106–11 in *Reweaving the Web of Life: Feminism and Nonviolence*. Philadelphia: New Society Publishers.

Krauss, Celene. 1993. "Women and Toxic Waste Protests: Race, Class and Gender as Resources of Resistance." *Qualitative Sociology* 16(3): 247–62.

Laslett, Barbara, Johanna Brenner, and Yesim Arat. 1995. "Feminists Rethink the Political." Pp. 1–8 in *Rethinking the Political: Gender Resistance and the State*. Chicago: The University of Chicago Press.

Liberation Support Movement (LSM). 1974. *The Mozambican Woman in the Revolution*. Richmond: LSM Information Center.

Lindsey, Linda. 1997. *Gender Roles: A Sociological Perspective*, 3^d ed. Upper Saddle River, N.J.: Prentice-Hall.

Lodge, Tom. 1983. *Black Politics in South Africa Since 1945*. Johannesburg: Raven Press.

Machel, Josina. 1974. "The Role of Women in the Revolution." Pp. 5–8 in *The Mozambican Woman in Revolution*. Richmond: Liberation Support Movement.

Macleod, Arlene Elowe. 1992. "Hegemonic Relations and Gender Resistance: The New Veiling as Accommodating Protest in Cairo." *Signs* 17(3).

Makamure, Nyaradzo. 1984. "Women and Revolution: The Women's Movement in Zimbabwe." *Journal of African Marxists* (6): 74–86.

Makhosikazi, Vukani. 1985. *South African Women on the Move*. London: Zed Books Ltd.

Margolis, Diane Rothbard. 1993. "Women's Movements around the World: Cross-Cultural Comparisons." *Gender and Society* 7(3): 379–99.

Marx, Gary T., and James L. Wood. 1975. "Strands of Theory and Research in Collective Behavior." *Annual Review of Sociology* 1: 363–428.

Marx, Gary T., and Douglas McAdam. 1994. *Collective Behavior and Social Movements: Process and Structure.* Englewood Cliffs, N.J.: Prentice-Hall.

Marx, Karl, Frederick Engels, V. I. Lenin, and Joseph Stalin. 1951. *The Woman Question.* New York: International Publishers.

McAdam, Doug, John D. McCarthy, and Mayer Zald. 1996. "Introduction: Opportunities, Mobilizing Structures, and Framing Processes—Toward a Synthetic, Comparative Perspective on Social Movements." Pp. 1–22 in *Comparative Perspectives on Social Movements: Political Opportunities, Mobilizing Structures, and Cultural Framings,* ed. Doug McAdam, John D. McCarthy, and Mayer N. Zald. New York: Cambridge University Press.

McAllister, Pam. 1982. *Reweaving the Web of Life: Feminism and Nonviolence.* Philadelphia: New Society Publishers.

Meer, Fatima. 1987. "Organizing Under Apartheid." Pp. 20–29 in *Third World— Second Sex,* vol. 2, ed. Miranda Davis. London: Zed Books Ltd.

Mies, Maria. 1986. *Patriarchy and Accumulation on a World Scale: Women in the International Division of Labour.* London: Zed Books, Ltd.

Moghadam, Valentine M. 1994. *Gender and National Identity: Women and Politics in Muslim Societies.* London: Zed Books, Ltd.

Molyneux, Maxine. 1981. "Socialist Societies Old and New: Progress towards Women's Emancipation." *Feminist Review* 8: 1–34.

Morgen, Sandra, and Ann Bookman. 1988. "Rethinking Women and Politics: An Introductory Essay." Pp. 3–32 in *Women and the Politics of Empowerment,* ed. Ann Bookman and Sandra Morgen. Philadelphia: Temple University Press.

Morrison, Minion K. C. 1987. *Black Political Mobilization: Leadership, Power, and Mass and Mass Behavior.* Albany, N.Y.: State University of New York Press.

Mueller, Carol. 1992. "Building Social Movement Theory." Pp. 3–25 in *Frontiers in Social Movement Theory,* ed. Aldon D. Morris and Carol McClurg Mueller. New Haven: Yale University Press.

———. 1994. "Conflict Networks and the Origins of Women's Liberation." Pp. 235–63 in *New Social Movements: From Ideology to Identity,* ed. Enrique Larana, Hank Johnston, and Joseph R. Gusfield. Philadelphia: Temple University Press.

Neft, Naomi, and Ann D. Levine. 1997. *Where Women Stand: An International Report on the Status of Women in 140 Countries.* New York: Random House.

Nicola-McLaughlin, Andree. 1988. "The International Nature of the Struggle of Southern African Women." *Network: A Pan-African Women's Forum* 1(1): 49–56.

Nnaemeka, Obioma, ed. 1998. *Sisterhood, Feminisms, and Power: From Africa to the Diaspora.* Trenton, N.J.: Africa World Press, Inc.

Oberschall, Anthony. 1973. *Social Conflicts and Social Movements.* Englewood Cliffs, N.J.: Prentice-Hall.

Oliver, Pamela. 1984. "'If You Don't Do It, Nobody Else Will': Active and Token Contributors to Local Collective Action." *American Sociological Review* 49: 601–10.

———. 1980. "Rewards and Punishments as Selective Incentives for Collective Action: Theoretical Investigations." *American Journal of Sociology* 84: 1256–75.

Oliver, Pamela E., and Gerald Marwell. 1988. "The Paradox of Group Size in Collective Action: A Theory of the Critical Mass II." *American Sociological Review* 53: 1–8.

Oliver, Pamela E., Gerald Marwell, and Ray Teixeria. 1985. "A Theory of the Critical Mass I, Interdependence, Group Heterogeneity, and the Production of Collective Action." *American Journal of Sociology* 91: 522–56.

Oppenheimer, Martin, and George Lakey. 1964. *A Manual for Direct Action*. Chicago: Quadrangle Books.

Orr, Leisl. 1999. "Research Report: Women's Leadership in COSATU." National Labour and Economic Development Institute, Johannesburg, South Africa.

Payne, Charles. 1989. "Ella Baker and Models of Social Change." *Signs* 14: 885–89.

———. 1998. "Debating the Civil Rights Movement: The View from the Trenches." Pp. 99–136 in *Debating the Civil Rights Movement, 1945–68*, Steven Lawson and Charles Payne. Lanham, Md.: Rowman and Littlefield Publishers, Inc.

Perkins, Margo V. 2000. *Autobiography as Activism: Three Black Women of the Sixties*. Jackson: University of Mississippi Press.

Peteet, Julie M. 1989. "Women and National Politics in the Middle East." Pp. 136–56 in *Power and Stability in the Middle East*, ed. Berch Berberoglu. London: Zed Books.

———. 1991. *Gender in Crisis: Women and the Palestinian Resistance Movement*. New York: Oxford University Press.

Pichado, Nelson A. 1988. "Resource Mobilization: An Analysis of Conflicting Theoretical Variations." *Sociological Quarterly* 29: 97–110.

Polletta, Francesca. 1997. "Culture and Its Discontents: Recent Theorizing on the Cultural Dimensions of Protest." *Sociological Inquiry* 67(4): 431–50.

Qunta, Christine, ed. 1987. *Women in Southern Africa*. London: Allison and Busby Limited.

Radcliffe, Sarah A., and Allie Westwood. 1993. *Viva: Women and Popular Protest in Latin America*. London: Routledge.

Ramphele, Mamphela. 1995. *Mamphela Ramphele: A Life*. Cape Town: David Philip.

Randall, Vicky. 1982. *Women and Politics*. New York: St Martin's Press.

Rochford, E. Burke. 1982. "Recruitment Strategies, Ideology, and Organization in the Hare Krishna Movement." *Social Problems* 29: 399–410.

Russell, Diana E. H. 1989. *Lives of Courage: Women for a New South Africa*. New York: BasicBooks.

Salem, Dorothy. 1990. *To Better Our World: Black Women in Organized Reform, 1890–1920*. Brooklyn, N.Y.: Carlson.

Schmink, Marianne. 1981. "Women in Brazilian Abertura Politics." *Journal of Women in Culture and Society* 7(11): 115–34.

Schwartz, Michael, and Shuva Paul. 1992. "Resource Mobilization versus the Mobilization of People." Pp. 205–23 in *Frontiers in Social Movement Theory*, ed. Aldon D. Morris and Carol McClurg Mueller. New Haven: Yale University Press.

Scott, James C. 1990. *Domination and the Arts of Resistance: Hidden Transcripts*. New Haven: Yale University Press.

Seeking, Jeremy. 1991. "Gender Ideology and Township Politics in the 1980s." *Agenda: A Journal about Women and Gender* 10: 77–88.

Seidman, Gay. 1984. "Women in Zimbabwe: Postindependence Struggles." *Feminist Studies* 10(3): 419–39.

Skolpol, Theda. 1979. *States and Social Revolutions*. Cambridge: Cambridge University Press.

Shaffer, Krista. 1997. "Septima Clark: Broadening Our Understandings of Education, Citizenship, and Teaching," Unpublished thesis. Durham, N.C.: Duke University.

Sherkat, Darren E., and T. Jean Blocker. 1994. "The Political Development of Sixties' Activists: Identifying the Influence of Class, Gender, and Socialization on Protest Participation." *Social Forces* 72(3): 821–42.

Smith, Barbara. 1983. *Home Girls: A Black Feminist Anthology.* New York: Kitchen Table: Women of Color Press.

Snow, David A. 1979. "A Dramaturgical Analysis of Movement Accommodation: Building Idiosyncrasy Credit as a Movement Mobilization Strategy." *Symbolic Interaction* 2: 23–44.

Staggenborg, Suzanne. 1998. *Gender, Family, and Social Movements.* Thousand Oaks, Calif.: Pine Forge Press.

Steady, Filomina Chioma. 1993. "Women and Collective Action: Female Models in Transition." Pp. 90–101 in *Theorizing Black Feminisms: The Visionary Pragmatism of Black Women*, ed. Stanlie M. James and Abena P. A. Busia. London: Routledge.

Tarrow, Sidney. 1996. "States and Opportunities: The Political Structuring of Social Movements." Pp. 41–61 in *Comparative Perspectives on Social Movements: Political Opportunities, Mobilizing Structures, and Cultural Framings*, ed. Doug McAdam, John D. McCarthy, and Mayer N. Zald. New York: Cambridge University Press.

Taylor, Verta, and Nancy Whittier. 1998. "Guest Editors' Introduction—Special Issue on Gender and Social Movements: Part 1." *Gender and Society* 12(6): 622–25.

———. 1999. "Guest Editors' Introduction: Special Issue on Gender and Social Movements: Part 2." *Gender and Society* 13(1): 5–7.

Terborg-Penn, Rosalyn, Sharon Harley, and Andrea Benton Rushing. 1987. *Women in Africa and the African Diaspora.* Washington, D.C.: Howard University Press.

Tetreault, Mary Ann, ed. 1994. *Women and Revolution in Africa, Asia, and the New World.* Columbia: University of South Carolina Press.

Thompson, Carol. 1982. "Women in the National Liberation Struggle in Zimbabwe: An Interview of Naomi Nhiwatiwa." *Women's Studies International Forum* 5(3/4): 247–52.

Turner, Ralph H. 1981. "Collective Behavior and Resource Mobilization as Appoaches to Social Movement: Issues and Continuities." Pp. 1–24 in *Research in Social Movements, Conflict, and Change*, vol. 4, ed. Louis Kreisberg. Greenwich, Conn.: JAI Press.

Turner, Ralph H., and Lewis M. Killian. 1957. *Collective Behavior.* Upper Saddle River, N.J.: Prentice-Hall.

Turok, Ben, ed. 1980. *Revolutionary Thought in the 20ᵗʰ Century.* London: Zed Books, Ltd.

Vogel, Lise. 1995. *Woman Questions: Essay for a Materialist Feminism.* London: Pluto Press.

Walker, Cherryl. 1990. *Women and Gender in Southern Africa to 1945.* Claremont, South Africa: David Philip.

Walsh, Edward J., and Rex H. Warland. 1983. "Social Movement Involvement in the Wake of a Nuclear Accident: Activists and Free Riders in the TMI Area." *American Sociological Review* 48(6): 764–80.

Wells, Julia C. 1983. "Why Women Rebel: A Comparative Study of South African Women's Resistance in Bloemfontein (1913) and Johannesburg (1958)." *Journal of Southern African Studies* 10(1): 55–70.

———. 1998. "Maternal Politics in Organizing Black South African Women: The Historical Lessons." Pp. 251–62 in *Sisterhood: Feminisms and Power from Africa to the Diaspora*, ed. Obioma Mnaemeka. Trenton, N.J.: African World Press.

West, Lois A. 1992. "Feminist Nationalist Social Movements: Beyond Universalism and Towards a Gendered Cultural Relativism." *Women's Studies International Forum* 15(5/6): 563–79.

———. 1997. *Feminist Nationalism*. New York. Routledge.

White, Deborah Gray. 1999. *Too Heavy a Load: Black Women in Defense of Themselves*. New York: Norton.

Whittier, Nancy. 1997. "Political Generations, Micro-cohorts, and the Transformation of Social Movements." *American Sociological Review* 62: 760–78.

Wilson, Kenneth, and Tony Orum. 1976. "Mobilizing People for Collective Political Action." *Journal of Political and Military Sociology* 4: 187–202.

Yuval-Davis, Nira, and Floya Anthias, eds. 1989. *Woman-Nation-State*. London: Macmillan Press.

Zald, Mayer N., and Roberta Ash. 1966. "Social Movement Organizations: Growth, Decay and Change." *Social Forces* 44: 327–41.

Zald, Mayer N., and John D. McCarthy, eds. 1979. *The Dynamics of Social Movements*. Cambridge: Winthrop.

M. Bahati Kuumba is currently Associate Professor of Women's Studies and Associate Director of the Women's Research and Resource Center at Spelman College. Prior to this appointment, Dr. Kuumba was Associate Professor of Sociology at Buffalo State College, where she taught for seven years and served as Coordinator of the African and African American Studies Interdisciplinary Unit and as a core committee member of the Women's Studies Interdisciplinary Unit. Her scholarly research focuses on women transnationally in the areas of social resistance movements, population policy, and feminist theory/praxis. She has conducted research on women and women's organizations in the United States, Cuba, Zimbabwe, and South Africa. Professor Kuumba has published in *Sociological Forum, Race, Gender, and Class, Africa Today*, and *Mobilization: The International Journal of Social and Political Movements*. She has also authored several book chapters on women and gender in cross-cultural and race/class/gender perspective. Her most recent scholarly work can be found in *Still Lifting, Still Climbing: African American Women's Contemporary Activism*, edited by Kimberly Springer (NYU Press, 1999). M. Bahati Kuumba is also a mother, cultural worker, and activist who has participated in the International Women's, Pan-African, Economic Justice, and Latin American and Anti-Apartheid Solidarity movements.